PUT OPTION STRATEGIES FOR SMARTER TRADING

PUT OPTION STRATEGIES FOR SMARTER TRADING

HOW TO PROTECT AND BUILD CAPITAL IN TURBULENT MARKETS

Michael C. Thomsett

Vice President, Publisher: Tim Moore
Associate Publisher and Director of Marketing: Amy Neidlinger
Executive Editor: Jim Boyd
Editorial Assistant: Pamela Boland
Operations Manager: Gina Kanouse
Senior Marketing Manager: Julie Phifer
Publicity Manager: Laura Czaja
Assistant Marketing Manager: Megan Colvin
Cover Designer: Chuti Prasertsith
Managing Editor: Kristy Hart
Project Editors: Julie Anderson and Jovana San Nicolas-Shirley
Copy Editor: Chuck Hutchinson
Proofreader: Williams Woods Publishing Services
Indexer: Michael C. Thomsett
Senior Compositor: Gloria Schurick
Manufacturing Buyer: Dan Uhrig

© 2010 by Pearson Education, Inc.
Publishing as FT Press
Upper Saddle River, New Jersey 07458

FT Press offers excellent discounts on this book when ordered in quantity for bulk purchases or special sales. For more information, please contact U.S. Corporate and Government Sales, 1-800-382-3419, corpsales@pearsontechgroup.com. For sales outside the U.S., please contact International Sales at international@pearson.com.

Company and product names mentioned herein are the trademarks or registered trademarks of their respective owners.

Printed in the United States of America

First Printing December 2009

ISBN-10: 0-13-701290-X
ISBN-13: 978-0-13-701290-9

Pearson Education LTD.
Pearson Education Australia PTY, Limited.
Pearson Education Singapore, Pte. Ltd.
Pearson Education North Asia, Ltd.
Pearson Education Canada, Ltd.
Pearson Educatioń de Mexico, S.A. de C.V.
Pearson Education—Japan
Pearson Education Malaysia, Pte. Ltd.

Library of Congress Cataloging-in-Publication Data

Thomsett, Michael C.

Put option strategies for smarter trading : how to protect and build capital in turbulent markets / Michael C. Thomsett.

p. cm.

Includes index.

ISBN 978-0-13-701290-9 (hardback : alk. paper) 1. Stock options. 2. Options (Finance) I. Title.

HG6042.T463 2010

332.63'2283—dc22

2009031909

CONTENTS

ACKNOWLEDGMENTS

My thanks to the many people who helped me in the preparation of this book. These include the staff at candlestickcharts.com who generously provided permission to use their materials within the book, and to the excellent editorial staff at Pearson Education and FT Press, especially executive editor Jim Boyd and project editor Julie Anderson.

Also thanks to the first-line editing by Linda Rose Thomsett, and to the professionals at the Chicago Board Options Exchange for their friendship, support and editorial guidance, most notably Marty Kearney and Jim Bittman.

ABOUT THE AUTHOR

Michael C. Thomsett is a widely published author with over 70 published books. He is especially known for his options publishing. His books include *Options Trading for the Conservative Investor* and *The Options Trading Body of Knowledge* (FT Press), *Winning with Options* (Amacom Books), *The LEAPS Strategist* (Marketplace Books) and the best-selling *Getting Started in Options* (John Wiley & Sons) which has sold over 250,000 copies and was released in 2009 in its 8th edition.

Thomsett also writes on many stock market investment topics. His *Investment and Securities Dictionary* (hardcover McFarland & Company and paperback Prentice Hall) was named by *Choice Magazine* as an Outstanding Academic Book of the Year. He also wrote *The Mathematics of Investing* (John Wiley & Sons), *The Stock Investor's Pocket Calculator* (Amacom) and *Stock Profits* (FT Press). The author lives near Nashville and writes fulltime. His Web site is www.MichaelThomsett.com.

INTRODUCTION

Surviving in Volatile and Falling Markets

Declining market value in stocks, alarming economic news, chronic housing and credit problems, uncertain oil prices—all these critical conditions that were worse than ever in 2008 and 2009 make the point that you need alternatives to survive in troubling economic times.

There is good news.

The options market is relatively young, but the popularity of options trading has grown exponentially every year since the early 1970s. This has occurred as increasing numbers of investors have realized that options are more than mere speculative tools. They are effective risk hedge instruments, cash generators, and portfolio management tools that virtually anyone can use beneficially. Even if you have very low risk tolerance, conservative options strategies can strengthen your portfolio and reduce market risks while generating current income.

In volatile markets, when you have no idea what stock values are going to be next month or even next week, options are especially valuable. In outright bear markets such as the market that started in 2007 and extended into 2009, put options offer a way to profit from declining stock values. This book is designed to explore a number of put strategies that can be used to provide profits when the markets are falling.

A *put* is an option designed to increase in value when the underlying security's value falls. It is the opposite of a *call*, which is better known as an instrument that tracks a stock's value and rises when the stock's price rises. Traders often overlook put options because so many are naturally optimistic by nature. It is a common pitfall to believe that a stock's value is always going to rise, and many investors treat their purchase price as a starting point from which values can only increase as time goes by. But anyone who was invested in the markets in 2008 and

2009 knows that this belief is flawed and also that it has expensive consequences. Stocks do fall in value. And when they do, it often defies logic. In 2008, rapid declines in stocks once thought to be invincible made the point that markets overreact. By the end of 2008, many stocks were available at bargain prices, but panic and fear were so widespread that few investors were brave enough to put capital into the equity markets.

This is the perfect market for option trading—and for a number of reasons. On a purely speculative approach to markets that have declined, low prices represent values; and when those prices bounce back (as they always do), anyone who got in at the lowest price levels makes handsome profits. However, if you are so concerned about declining stocks that you do not want to invest in shares, options provide attractive alternatives. The same is true when markets peak at the top. Overbought markets invariably correct; so if you don't want to take profits, but you are concerned about declining values over the short term, options can be used to protect stock positions without having to sell shares.

There are so many possible uses for options and specifically for puts that you can take advantage of the potential in any kind of market. Whether prices are depressed or inflated, and whether the mood is bull or bear, puts are effective devices for maximizing profits. In volatile and falling markets, the value of puts is at a maximum. This is true because the mood in the markets is always fearful at such times. When market prices are rising rapidly, euphoria and even unjustified optimism rule, and in these conditions, putting money at risk is easy. But on the opposite side of the spectrum, when prices are low, doom and despair are the ruling emotions; and few people are willing to put money at risk in this environment.

All markets are cyclical, and that is why using puts as portfolio management devices should remain flexible. The most depressing market, whether in stocks, real estate, credit, or housing, is eventually going to come back and improve. When at the worst portion of a cycle, the situation always seems permanent, and investors cannot see their way to a recovery. But recovery does occur, and it always takes the markets by surprise. By the end of 2008, the P/E ratio of stocks on the S&P 500 had fallen from 26 three months earlier to about 18, a decline of more than 30 percent.[1]

This fall in the overall market's P/E ratio defines the bear market of the time. This ratio, which tracks market sentiment about the future price direction of stocks, is far lower than it was only four years earlier when it peaked above 40; but many people are surprised to learn that the dismal 2008 numbers were higher than historical averages. A few decades ago in the 1970s, S&P 500 P/E fell into single digits and did not rise above 20 until the mid-1980s; so the decline in this important benchmark by the end of 2008 demonstrated that the current market is not as severe or as depressed as it has been in the recent past.

All these historical trends, when viewed in perspective, make the point that even the most volatile current market needs to be analyzed in context. Most market cycles last between two and five years, and the longer the downturn, the more rapid the recovery seems to be. Past cycles have demonstrated this interesting tendency time and again. What this means for investors is that volatility and uncertainty—as troubling as they are—present opportunities as well. And using puts to take advantage of volatility can be quite profitable in several ways:

- Producing short-term profits simply by timing buy and sell decisions based on rapid and volatile price changes;
- Protecting long stock positions by using puts as a form of insurance for paper profits;
- Entering into contingent purchase positions of stock using puts rather than committing funds; and
- Employing a variety of combined strategies to hedge risk while producing short-term profits and leveraged control over stock.

This book explains all the put-based strategies in detail and shows how even a troubled market presents great opportunities to keep you in control. The worst aspect of volatile markets is a sense of not having control over events, and puts can be used to offset this apprehension. You have probably heard that astute traders can earn profits in all types of markets. Puts are among the best devices to accomplish that goal.

---

[1] Source: BullandBearWise, at www.bullandbearwise.com/SPEarningsChart.asp

1

THE FLEXIBLE NATURE OF OPTIONS: RISKS FOR ALL LEVELS

A re you investing in companies or in the prices of their stock? A lot of emphasis is placed on the difference between "value" and "growth," but perhaps a more important distinction should be made between what you invest in. If you follow the fundamentals, you are probably investing in the company; if you are a technician, your interest is in the stock and its price movement.

In either case, buying and selling stock are not the only alternatives you have. In fact, the volatility of the market, by itself, makes the case that just using a buy-and-hold strategy is very high risk when markets are volatile. All you need to do is to compare prices of some of the best-known companies between the end of 2007 and 2008 to see what a disastrous market that 12-month period was. This includes 28 out of 30 stocks on the Dow Jones Industrial Average, which all lost value.[1]

When you buy shares of stock, you enter into a rigid contract. You pay money for shares, and those shares either increase or decrease in value. You are entitled to dividends if the company has declared and paid them. And if you own common stock, you have the right to vote on corporate matters put forth by the board of directors. The stock remains in existence for as long as you want to continue owning shares, and you have the right to sell those shares whenever you wish.

---

[1] In 2008, only two Dow companies—McDonald's and Wal-Mart—gained in value. The other 28 DJIA stocks all fell.

With options, the contract is quite different. An option controls 100 shares of stock but costs much less. However, holding an option grants no voting rights and no dividends (unless you also own the stock). You can close an option position at any time you want on listed options on stock. But perhaps the most important distinction between stock and options is that options have only a finite life. They expire at a specified date in the future. After expiration, the option is worthless. So it has to be closed or exercised before expiration to avoid losing all its value. You exercise a put by selling 100 shares at the fixed strike price, and you exercise a call by buying 100 shares at the fixed strike price.

> **Key Point:** Stock and option terms are quite different, including indefinite versus finite lives, dividends, and voting rights.

Options, in general, contain specific *terms* defining their value and status. These terms include the type of option (put or call), the underlying security, the strike price, and expiration date. Every option's terms are distinct; listed option terms cannot be changed or exchanged other than by closing one option and replacing it with another.

Terms of Options

The terms of each option contract define it and set value (known as premium) for each and every option contract. These terms are described next.

Types of Options

There are two kinds of options: puts and calls. A put grants its owner the right, but not the obligation, to *sell* 100 shares of a specific underlying security, at a fixed strike price, and before the specified expiration date. A seller of a put may be obligated to buy 100 shares at the fixed strike price, which occurs when the market value of stock is lower than the put's strike price.

A call is the opposite. If you buy a call, you have the right, but not the obligation, to *buy* 100 shares of a specific underlying security, at a fixed strike price, and before the specified expiration date. A seller of a call may be obligated to sell 100 shares at the fixed strike price, which occurs when the market value of stock is higher than the call's strike price.

> **Key Point:** Holders of long positions are not obligated to exercise, but their positions give them leveraged control over 100 shares of stock per contract.

The rights and obligations of option buyers and sellers are summarized in Figure 1.1.

Option rights and obligations

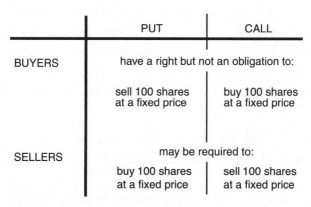

Figure 1.1 Option rights and obligations

Put values rise if the underlying security's share price falls. This occurs because the fixed strike price does not change; so the lower the current price of the stock, the more valuable the right to sell 100 shares at the higher strike price. For a call, the value rises when the underlying security price increases; so the higher the current price of the stock, the more valuable the right to buy 100 shares at the lower strike price.

For example, if you buy a put with a strike price of 35 and the stock's market value falls to $28 per share, you gain a 7-point advantage. You can sell 100 shares of stock at the strike price of $35, or $700 higher than the current market value of the stock. If you buy a call with a strike price of $40 and the stock's market value rises to $44 per share, your call grants you the right to buy 100 shares at the strike price of $40, or $400 below current market value.

These basic attributes of options form the rationale for all strategies, whether they involve one or more option positions, short or long, and combinations of various kinds (options hedged against stock positions, combinations of call with call, call with put, or put with put in a variety of long or short positions and employing one or many different strike prices.) The strategic possibilities are endless and provide hedging and insurance for many positions and in many different kinds of markets.

Underlying Security

The underlying security may be 100 shares of stock, an index, or a futures position. This book limits examples to options on stock, which are the most popular in the options market and also the most likely kind of underlying security most people will use for option trading. The underlying cannot be changed. Once you open a long or short option position, it is tied to the underlying and will gain or lose value based on the direction the stock moves.

> **Key Point:** Every option position relates to a specific underlying security, and this is not transferable.

The underlying may have a fairly narrow trading range, or it may be quite volatile. The degree of price volatility in the underlying (market risk) also affects option premium values. The greater the volatility, the greater the value of the option. This volatility premium, also called *extrinsic* value, will change as expiration date approaches; but for longer-term options, the volatility of the underlying is a significant portion of total premium value. So the attributes of the underlying are essential for judging the value of options. It is a mistake to determine which options to buy or sell based solely on their current value; the quality of a company on a fundamental basis and the price volatility of its stock (or its technical risk attributes) have to be compared and judged as well to make an informed trade decision.

Strike Price

Strike price is the fixed price at which an option can be exercised. The strike price determines total option value. The proximity between strike and the current value of each share of stock determines whether premium value is growing or shrinking. When a put's strike is higher than the current market value of the underlying stock, it is *in the money*; and when a call's strike is lower than the current market value of the underlying stock, it is also in the money. If the stock's price moves above the put's strike or below the call's strike, the option is *out of the money*. If stock share price and the option's strike price are exactly the same, the option is *at the money*.

> **Key Point:** The proximity between strike price and current market value of the underlying determines the premium values of every option.

These relationships between strike of the option and current value of the underlying security are summarized in Figure 1.2.

option status

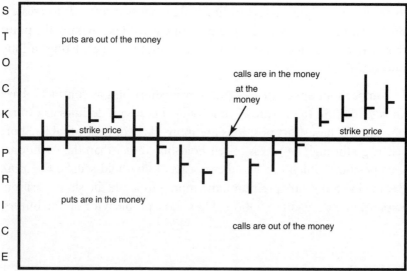

Figure 1.2   Option status

Expiration Date

An option's expiration date is fixed and cannot be changed. It occurs after the third Friday of the expiration month. Standard listed options expire up to eight months out, and the longer-terms option (LEAPS, or Long-term Equity Anticipation Securities) expire up to 30 months away, always in January.

The time to expiration determines how options are valued. The longer the time, the greater the portion of an option's premium known as *time value*. It may be quite high when options have many months to go before they expire, but as expiration nears, the decline in time value accelerates. By expiration day, time value falls to zero.

> **Key Point:** The fact that options expire means value is also finite; unlike stock, every option becomes worthless as soon as the expiration date has passed.

For option buyers, time is a problem. If you buy an option with a long time until expiration date, you will have to pay for that time in higher premium; and if expiration will occur in the near future, premium is lower, but the rapid decline in time value makes it difficult to create a profit. Three-quarters of all options expire worthless, making the point that it is very difficult to beat the odds simply by speculating in long puts or calls.

In comparison, option sellers (those who short option contracts) have an advantage in the nature of time value. Because it declines as expiration approaches, short positions are more likely to be profitable. Short sellers go through a process of sell-hold-buy rather than the traditional long position, which involves the process of buy-hold-sell. So the more decline in an option's premium, the more profitable the short position. Expiration is a benefit to option sellers and a problem for option buyers.

Valuation of Options

Every option has an overall value, known as its premium. But the total premium consists of three specific parts: intrinsic value, time value, and extrinsic value. The first two are quite easy to understand, but extrinsic value is where all the variations are going to be found. For example, if you look at two stocks with the same market value and with options for the same strike and expiration, you are still going to find differences in those option premiums. The reasons are explained by extrinsic value.

Intrinsic Value

The option's intrinsic value is easy to understand. It is the point value equal to the option's in-the-money level. For example, a 30 put has three points of intrinsic value when the underlying stock is at $27 per share ($30 - $27 = $3). If the stock's value is higher than the put's strike, there is no intrinsic value.

> **Key Point:** Intrinsic value is equal to the number of points between strike price and current market value above (for a call) or below (for a put).

A call has intrinsic value whenever the underlying stock is higher than the call's strike. For example, if the strike is 45 and the current value of the underlying is $51 per share, the call has six points of intrinsic value ($51 - $45 = $6).

Intrinsic value will always track with the underlying stock's price movement. For a put, the intrinsic value increases point-for-point as the stock value falls; and for a call, intrinsic value increases point-for-point as the stock's value rises.

Although intrinsic value is easily defined and understood in the sense that it moves point-for-point with the underlying, the *total* premium does not always change exactly with price changes. The variation occurs because of the nature of extrinsic value (explained later). When you see a stock's price move by three points and the option change by only two or perhaps by four points, the explanation involves an offset between intrinsic and extrinsic value. So although intrinsic value does change predictably, total premium may offset that movement because of price adjustments made in extrinsic value. The risk and volatility of the stock, time to expiration, and changing technical information about the company all have an effect in extrinsic value.

Time Value

Time value is just as easy to track as intrinsic value. The longer the time to expiration, the higher the time value. As expiration approaches, time value declines and the rate of decline accelerates as expiration nears. So there is going to be very little change in time value for a LEAPS option with two years to expiration, and a very rapid deterioration of time value during an option's last two months of life.

Option buyers struggle with time value, because declining premium levels make it difficult if not impossible to build profits in long option positions. For example, if you buy an out-of-the-money put for 3 ($300) and with six months until expiration, you need the underlying to move down by three points in-the-money (below strike) just to break even by expiration; and it has to move even further to make any profit.

> **Key Point:** Like intrinsic value, time value is predictable and specific; it declines as expiration approaches, ending up at zero.

Option sellers benefit from declining time value for the same reasons. For example, if you sell an out-of-the-money put for 3 ($300) and with six months until expiration, you need the underlying to move only by less than three points in the money to make a profit. Because none of the premium is intrinsic, as long as the stock remains at or above the put's strike, it is easy to profit from declining time value at any time before expiration.

Extrinsic Value

Of the three types of premium in an option, extrinsic value is the most interesting and the most complex. It is a reflection of the price volatility (market risk) of the underlying stock. The more volatility, the higher the extrinsic value as a rule. But the longer the time to expiration, the more variation you will find in intrinsic value. It is even possible that increases in intrinsic value will be offset by declines in extrinsic value— due simply to the fact that a lot can happen in an extended period of time.

For example, you buy a put LEAPS with 24 months until expiration. Strike is 25 and the stock currently is at $25 per share (at the money). Total premium is 7 ($700). You believe the stock's market value will decline and create a profit in coming months; you are also aware that the entire premium consists of nonintrinsic value. Over the following month, the underlying declines to $21, a drop of four points in the money. However, the option premium grows only to 9, a change of two points.

> **Key Point:** Extrinsic value is the only form of option value that is uncertain, and that varies based on underlying market risk and volatility.

In this case, two things have occurred. There is little or no change in time value because the time to expiration is so far off. Intrinsic value increased by four points ($25 - $21 = $4); but extrinsic value fell by two points (4 - 2 = 2). This offset is an odd combination of factors. It contains the influence of time and volatility. With 24 months remaining until expiration, the offset between intrinsic and extrinsic value is a way that the market questions whether that particular option should be priced for the entire amount of intrinsic change. While the adjustment is made to intrinsic value, time has a lot to do with this offset; if there was less time remaining in the life of the put, the offset would not be as severe and, in fact, it might not occur at all.

Extrinsic value plays a role in option premium that modifies the effects of both intrinsic and time value. Neither of those portions of the option premium change as part of this price adjustment. Because intrinsic and time value are specific and exact, the change is extrinsic only. Remember, both intrinsic and time value are predictable. Intrinsic value reflects the number of points in the money (so when the option is at the money or out of the money, there is zero intrinsic value). And time value changes on a time-based curve and does not change over time. Time value is affected solely by the proximity of expiration.

Even though these rules are specific, extrinsic value is affected by both the degree of intrinsic change and the time until expiration. This complexity explains why a longer-term in-the-money option premium does not exactly track changes in the underlying; it also explains why even out-of-the-money options are often quite unresponsive to changes in the underlying. For example, a long-term put that is out-of-the-money might have little or no change in the premium even when the underlying moves closer to the strike price level. The unresponsiveness of the option premium in long-term out-of-the-money status makes sense because you cannot expect more point-for-point changes until (a) expiration is much closer and (b) the option is in the money.

> **Key Point:** Although extrinsic and time value are not the same, the variation in extrinsic value often is affected by the time remaining until expiration.

The variation between degrees of stock price change and option premium change is called *implied volatility* and defines option values when they do occur. An option's premium is almost always worth at least its intrinsic value, and in cases in which it falls below that benchmark, it is going to be very temporary. Because both intrinsic and time value are specific, any bargains in option pricing are going to be found in adjustments to extrinsic value, known as an evolving trend in the option's implied volatility.

Dividends and Puts

Most traders who buy calls know that dividends have a negative impact on premium value. This occurs when the stock goes ex-dividend, the day when the dividend is factored into the share price. However, while this is a negative factor for call buyers, it is a positive one for put buyers.

Since dividends reduce the share value of stock, in-the-money calls are expected to also lose value. But because puts increase in value as stock price falls, an in-the-money put will *increase* in value at ex-dividend date. This reality may affect the timing of many put strategies. Knowing in advance that the put's value will fall because ex-dividend date is looming builds in extra premium appreciation beyond the normal cause and effect of price change in the underlying. The strategy of timing with a dividend in mind is the same for long puts as it is for short calls; a decline in the stock price is predictable, so the long put will increase in value (beneficial to its owner or buyer) and the short call will decline in value (beneficial to the seller).

> **Key Point:** Whereas dividends are a detriment to call buyers because stock prices fall as a result, they are a benefit to put buyers. The decline in underlying value is offset by an increase in the put's premium value.

Dividends are often overlooked as a factor in both the selection of options and the timing of trades. This is a mistake; dividends represent a significant portion of potential profits on both stock trades and option trades. For example, if you select a stock paying a relatively high dividend (4 percent, for example), ownership of the stock includes an ensured 4 percent annual return. This is even greater if the dividends are reinvested in partial shares, which converts the nominal rate into a compound rate of return.

Dividend income is also significant when considering the relative value and likely outcome of a put strategy that includes ownership of stock. You earn dividends only if you own shares of stock, so this extra consideration applies only when strategies include long stock positions in conjunction with long or short positions. When you compare likely outcome in a number of scenarios, include dividend income in the equation.

For example, you may construct an option strategy combining a long stock position with either long or short puts, or with puts and calls in spread or straddle positions. If you are looking at several different companies as potential candidates for such a strategy, including the dividend income often makes a substantial difference. Assuming that the assumed value of each issue is comparable, a dividend-paying stock is likely to produce a better overall yield than a stock that does not pay a dividend (or one paying a much smaller dividend).

In coming chapters, return calculations include dividend income as a means for comparison. For example, if three different stocks using the same strategy are assumed to produce a range of returns between 7 and

8 percent, a 3 percent dividend on one stock will make it the clear winner in overall income.

Besides augmenting total income from a combined stock and option strategy, dividends create a cushion of downside protection in the stock position. Stocks held for many years grow significantly in value when quarterly dividends are reinvested and when additional income is generated through option strategies. Many of these combined strategies are quite low risk and may produce consistent cash income representing double-digit returns (including dividends), but with little added market risk when compared to simply owning shares of stock.

Comparing Risk Levels

Any option strategy should be analyzed with risk in mind. Any single-option long position contains a specific market risk, based on the fact that most are going to expire worthless or be closed at a net loss. The effects of declining time value make it very difficult to profit from buying options for speculation.

Many additional reasons for buying puts can justify the market risk. For example, protecting paper profits in appreciated stock by buying puts provides a form of insurance. If the stock price does retreat, appreciated put value offsets the decline in value; the put can be closed at a profit to recapture the paper profits lost; or it can even be exercised. This allows you to sell 100 shares of stock for each put owned, at the fixed strike price. So as long as the strike is higher than current market value, this type of long put position hedges the stock position. In a volatile market, this can be a valuable strategic move; it can make long stock positions more acceptable even with high volatility in the market because potential losses are insured against as long as the put position remains open.

> **Key Point:** The many specialized uses of long puts make them more than speculative in nature. They can reduce or eliminate risk in long stock holdings and work as an affordable market risk hedge.

Additional advanced strategies combining long puts with stock, with short puts, or with calls can also make the long put valuable as a source for potential profits or as a means for limiting risk in the overall position. So puts serve as a device for reducing profits in numerous stock and combined option positions.

Risk comparison should also be made between short puts and short calls. Writing naked calls is one of the highest-risk option strategies because, in theory, a stock's market price can rise indefinitely. This means that the true risk of a naked call is unknown. It is defined as the difference between market value of the stock and the short call's strike price, minus the call's premium received when the position was opened:

(current value, 100 shares - strike price, short call) = short call risk

This is "unlimited" because you cannot know how high the current price per share is going to reach. So uncovered calls are high risk. In comparison, a *covered* call is not only low risk; it is exceptionally conservative. By definition, a call is usually covered when you also own 100 shares of the underlying. In the event of exercise, you simply give up the 100 shares of stock at the strike price. So as long as the strike is higher than your original basis in the call, you profit with exercise from three sources: capital gain on the stock, premium on the short call, and dividends. Covered calls produce annualized returns in double digits in many cases because time value decline translates to higher profits for the call seller.

A short call is also "covered" when you own a long call that expires on the same date or later, and at the same strike. If the strike is higher, the risk is limited to the difference between the two strikes. For example, if you sell a May 55 call and buy a May 60 call, upon exercise you would exchange 100 shares at 60 for 100 shares at 55; your risk is limited to five points ($500). So a "covered" call based on short and long positions is usually only a partial reduction of risk. The difference in strikes combined with the net credit or debit normally translates to a net risk, but a relatively small one.

Key Point: A short call can be covered by ownership of 100 shares of stock, or by ownership of a long call expiring at the same date or a later date than the short position.

Short puts also contain risks and cannot be truly covered in the same way as calls. This means that while a short call is covered with 100 shares of long stock, a short put is not as easily made lower risk. However, short puts are not as risky as short calls, a fact often overlooked by those who want to go short on options. A short call may end up in a loss position, but the loss is not indefinite. A stock can fall only to zero, so a lower strike price represents a lower "worst case" risk. In a practical sense, the true risk of a short put is not really zero; it is actually the tangible book value of the stock. For example, if a stock is selling today at $34 per share and tangible book value per share (net worth less intangible assets) is $11 per share, the true maximum risk is $23, before considering the put premium received when the position is opened. If you receive a premium of 4 ($400) when you sell a put, the net tangible risk is 19 points:

$$(\$34 - \$11) - 4 = 19 \ (\$1,900)$$

If the entire premium is nonintrinsic (meaning the stock's market value was at or higher than the strike when the put is sold), this maximum risk is quite unlikely. As time moves on and expiration approaches, time value falls and the short put loses value.

Risk is further mitigated by rolling techniques. If the short put does go in the money, exercise can be avoided by closing the position or by rolling it forward. Short call sellers roll forward to a later exercise date, or forward and *up* to a higher strike to avoid exercise; short put positions are rolled forward to a later exercise date, or forward and *down* to a lower strike. Although rolling extends the period of exposure, it can result in an additional credit while avoiding exercise.

Considering the limited risk between strike and tangible book value per share, the decline in time value, and the ability to avoid exercise through rolling, short puts—often considered high-risk strategies—are actually not that high risk. This is especially true when the short put is combined with other stock and option positions, which are explored in detail in later chapters.

> **Key Point:** Uncovered call risk is unlimited and cannot be known; uncovered put risk is finite because the underlying can fall only so far.

The point to keep in mind about risks and puts is that strategies can be devised and designed to match your risk tolerance quite well. The purpose to any strategy should be understood and carefully articulated. In a volatile market, puts can be used to protect long stock positions, take advantage of exceptionally wild price gyrations, or simply to speculate on a rapidly changing market. For management of your portfolio, short and long puts serve many purposes and, when used appropriately to reduce risks, hedge other positions, or maximize income opportunities, can enhance profits while holding risks to a minimum.

Many stockholders have a sense of helplessness when markets become volatile, especially when the volatility takes market-wide prices to the downside. Widespread apprehension keeps many people out of the markets, awaiting further developments even if that means missing exceptional opportunities. Using puts in place of adding new positions to a depressed portfolio not only makes sense financially, but also enables you to control stock without needing to commit funds, protect paper profits, and create short-term profits even in the most unpredictable markets.

The next chapter examines risk hedge as a basic put strategy and shows how proper use of puts offset (and in many cases entirely remove) risk from other portfolio positions.

2

PUTS, THE OTHER OPTIONS: THE OVERLOOKED RISK HEDGE

Most investors are optimists. They assume their stocks are going to rise in value, starting from the moment they invest. In fact, many think of their basis price as the *zero point* of the investment, and prices are going to move upward from there. The reality—that the price you pay is part of a never-ending give and take between buyers and sellers—is that prices can move both up and down. For many, this presents a problem. What if the price does go down? Doesn't that mean you lose money? No. With options, you can profit in any kind of market, whether stock prices rise or fall, and even when prices don't move at all. Put-based strategies can limit losses, protect paper profits, and combine with other stock and option positions to create profits no matter what direction the market takes.

With so much focus on strategies involving calls, the options market as a whole may easily ignore the potential for puts, both as speculative devices and for managing a long stock portfolio. When employed to hedge risk, puts enable you to maintain holdings even when markets are volatile to the downside. The alternative—selling off stock positions out of fear of further declines—leads to lost opportunities. The classic outcome—selling stock to avoid further losses only to miss the rebound—is probably the most common timing problem for investors. Puts can eliminate this market risk.

The adage "Buy low and sell high" should contain a second part—"instead of the opposite." The tendency is to buy into the market top in the belief that prices will continue rising indefinitely, and sell into the bottom in fear or even panic that prices will continue their downward spiral. Puts are useful in both of these situations. Buying long puts at the market bottom can be done to take advantage of a rebound; it may also be done as a means for offsetting lost opportunities after selling stock.

For example, a market decline leaves stock valued far below its original purchase price. Fearing further declines, you sell shares to cut losses. But concerned about the timing of a possible rebound, you sell puts (or buy calls). In a sense, this is a hedge against lost opportunity and a way to recapture losses from sold stock, if and when prices do return. However, the risk factor cannot be ignored. You have no way of knowing whether the price of the underlying will continue to fall, meaning the short put may be exercised. The long call contains problems as well; you cannot know the timing of a price rebound, and given the finite life of a call, the risk that it will expire before it becomes possible to profit from the position is unavoidable.

Puts as Insurance for Paper Profits

At a price top, you can use long puts (or short calls) to protect paper profits, which provides a form of insurance in the event of a price correction. The popular strategy involves buying one long put per 100 shares of the underlying held in the portfolio. If the stock price does fall, the long put's intrinsic value will rise for each point lost in the stock, offsetting losses. The put can then be sold at a profit or exercised to sell shares at the strike price above current market value.

> **Key Point:** Puts can be used to protect paper profits; for each point the stock falls, an in-the-money long put's intrinsic value rises by one point.

The essence of this strategy is to limit or offset stock paper losses by corresponding gains in the put. For example, you own 100 shares of stock that you originally purchased at $44 per share. The most recent price is $53 per share and you do not want to sell; however, you are concerned about the potential for loss of the nine points of paper profits if the stock price does correct. You buy a 50 put expiring in five months and pay a premium of 2 ($200). Without the put, you would be at risk to lose the entire paper profit; if the stock price declined to your original purchase price of $44 per share and you then sold those shares, you would have no profit on the investment. Looking at this scenario another way, you would lose $900 in paper profits you could have taken by selling shares at the highest price, or $53 per share.

You may not want to sell shares for many reasons. Assuming you believe in the company's long-term prospects for further growth, holding shares may be very desirable. You may also want to avoid short-term capital gains on the stock, desiring to hold on for a longer period. A word of caution: If you buy a long put as a hedge for long shares and you have held the stock for less than the one-year period to gain long-term holding status, the holding period is lost and will not begin again until the put has been closed; so there is a tax consequence to the put when you have owned stock for less than one year. If you have owned stock for more than one year, you retain the long-term status upon sale of the stock.

An alternative to selling stock at its peak or hoping the price does not decline is to buy one put for 100 shares of stock. In the preceding example, the strike price is 50 (versus current market value of $53 per share) and the premium cost of the put is 2 ($200). So the worst-case outcome is a loss of $500 against the potential profit at the peak price of $53 per share. Realistically, the maximum loss is only $200 because unrealized profits do not count unless stock is sold. So even if the stock price fell below the original purchase price of $44 per share, intrinsic value of the put would be equal to the point difference between 50 and the current value of stock. This fixes a net profit of at least four points in the stock position, or nearly one-half of the total paper profits of nine points:

Strike price	$50
Original purchase price	44
Intrinsic value of the put	$ 6
Less: cost of the long put	2
Net profit	$ 4

So in a worst-case outcome, spending $200 to buy the put insurance ensures a net profit of $400 or more in the event of a price decline. The appreciated value of stock, or nine points, can also be almost entirely insured in this situation using the same put contract but buying two contracts per 100 shares. This 2-to-1 ratio insurance strategy guarantees at least eight points, or $800:

Strike price	$50
Original purchase price	44
Intrinsic value of one put	$ 6
Multiplied by two put contracts	× 2
Total intrinsic value	$12
Less: cost of the long puts	4
Net profit	$ 8

This protects eight of the nine points of paper profits at the peak in the worst-case outcome. However, if the stock price remains above $50 per share until expiration of the puts, the entire put premium is lost. And if you owned the stock for less than 12 months, you would also lose the accumulated time toward long-term status for the stock's capital gain.

> **Key Point:** Long put risk is always limited to the premium; however, potential gains are impressive when the timing and price movement work out.

If you purchase one put per 100 shares at the time of the original purchase, you create a hedge that may be very desirable. For a limited cost of opening a long put, you limit the downside risk while leaving intact the upside appreciation potential. Downside risk consists of two elements. First is the difference between purchase price and strike price; if the purchase price is higher than the strike, the point difference represents potential downside loss. For example, if you buy stock at $37 per share and buy a put with a 35 strike, you accept two points of downside risk. The second element is the cost of the put. So if the put costs 4 ($400), the total downside risk is limited to six points. Even if the stock falls far below the put strike, this is the maximum loss you would experience. On the upside, the cost of the put—$200—represents an added cost for the overall position. So the purchase price of stock is $37 per share, but your overall basis is equal to $39 per share including the cost of the put.

Most investors who add shares of stock to their portfolio do not consider the downside risk as part of the initial equation. If you believe the stock has the potential to rise based on a study of the company's fundamentals or of the stock's technical attributes, you would assume the price will rise, not fall. This is why put insurance is more common in situations in which you already own the stock and want to protect paper profits, versus insuring the original purchase price. Considering the potential tax problems associated with loss of the time count toward long-term gains, the put insurance strategy is most appropriate if you have already held shares long enough to qualify for long-term capital gains treatment of profits.

The risks to this strategy include not only the potential tax consequences when you are in short-term status (ownership under one year). A more serious risk is the premium cost of buying the put. For those who continually fear loss of paper profits, buying puts, waiting until expiration, and then buying more puts erodes profits and brings into question a larger issue: Should you remain invested in long stock if you continually fear a loss of paper profits? It may be more prudent to either sell shares and take profits when they are available, or adopt a longer-term point of view. If the reasons for buying the stock were sound at the time of purchase, it may be wise to ignore short-term price trends and hold for the long term. Even in that strategy, you can continue to protect profits by selling covered calls, or using long options to swing trade on the stock (see Chapter 4, "Swing Trading with Puts: Long and Short or Combined with Calls").

Selecting the Best Long Put

If using long puts for insurance makes sense, the question remains, which put should you pick? You will be concerned with three elements: time to expiration, strike, and cost.

> **Key Point:** For most insurance puts, the two major considerations are time to expiration and cost.

The selection of the "best" long put depends on several factors, including the length of time you believe you will need the insurance. If you are trying to time your open positions to avoid selling shares in the current tax year, remember the limitation regarding short-term holding periods. Also be aware of the wash rule, which recognizes a 30-day period both before and after a sale. Consult with a tax expert before entering into a strategy meant to affect tax liabilities before you make the move. In the next chapter, an expanded exploration of the insurance put expands this discussion to explain how proximity between the current price of stock and the strike price makes put selection even more important.

In picking the appropriate put for insurance of paper profits, you need to be aware not only of the purpose in making the decision, but also of the balance of the time, strike, and cost aspects to each possible contract.

For example, when McDonald's (MCD) had a market value of about $59.50 per share, the 52-week price range was between $46 and $67. Assuming you had bought 100 shares 12 months or more prior to this date and at a cost of $45, which put should you pick today to protect your 14.5 points of paper profits? (Remember, too, that although the example may no longer be applicable due to changing market values of all stocks, the relative value and timing of options and their underlying will always be approximately the same given the same levels of volatility.)

A sampling of puts with strikes of 57.50 and 60 are shown in Table 2.1 when the stock was at $59.50 per share.

Table 2.1 McDonald's (MCD) Puts

Expiration	Strike	Premium
JAN	57.50	0.05
JAN	60	0.75
FEB	57.50	1.91
FEB	60	2.95
MAR	57.50	3
MAR	60	4.10
JUN	57.50	5.90
JUN	60	6.20

Note that, understandably, the put premiums are higher when expiration is further away. This is a reflection of time value. The greater time periods provide more protection but cost more. Because the date of these values was mid-January, most people will reject the January puts as expiring too soon. February, also, would provide only one month of protection and, given the premium levels, it is questionable whether buying puts would be worthwhile. This is especially true for a stock like McDonald's, which was one of 2008's best performers in a very weak market. March and June contracts are more viable, but given the space of three months between the two expiration dates, the June contracts may seem the most practical.

> **Key Point:** There is always a connection between time to expiration and the cost of the put. Balancing these variables is essential in selecting the best put.

Next, analyze the premium differences between the two strikes being compared. The strike gap is 2.50 points, but the difference in put premiums is only 0.30 ($30). The June 60 put is the best choice in this field, assuming the premium level is acceptable and that you do not believe the stock's price is likely to fall in the immediate future (by February or March expirations). For a premium of 6.20 ($620), you protect the $60 per share price.

To analyze this from the point of view of your basis: You bought the stock at $45 per share more than 12 months ago. So you have the long-term capital gains status locked in, even if you sell. That is a 15.50-point assured gain on the stock, but at the cost of $620 for the put; the guaranteed net profit in this example is $930 ($1550 − $620). To critically evaluate this strategy, you also need to ask yourself whether you believe the stock is at risk of falling *more* than 6.20 points in the near future. If this seems unlikely, why buy the put? It would make sense only if you want to hold the stock for the long term, you have faith in its continuing technical price strength, and you are not concerned with short-term price swings.

In the alternative, you could place a stop-loss order for a price in between the current level of $59.50 per share and the price 6.20 points

---

lower, or $53.30 per share. The $53.30 value is the current value minus the cost of the insurance put. So if you do not buy the insurance put and place a stop-loss order at $55 per share, you achieve a better level of protection in the event of a significant and rapid price decline, but for no cost. This is a sound idea unless you simply do not want to sell shares in any situation. Then you should consider one of the alternatives:

- Buy the insurance put.
- Take no action because you want to hold for the long term.
- Sell covered calls to generate current income (thus discounting your net basis and generating cash).
- Swing trade with both long calls and long puts if and when price swings are extreme in the short term.

> **Key Point:** You *always* have alterna-
> tives in using options in your portfolio.
> It is invariably a wise move to consider
> all these options before picking one.

Insurance puts should be used only when you find a good value and when you want to hedge against price volatility in the underlying. If you do not want to risk having shares sold automatically (via a stop-loss order, for example), the insurance put may serve as a good measure in managing paper profits. Creating a ratio makes more sense when multiple lots of 100 shares are involved. The example of a 2-to-1 ratio involving two puts for 100 shares increases potential offset of loss in the underlying, but with a substantially higher cost. The relative cost in exchange for hedging benefit becomes more practical with three puts per 200 shares (3-to-2 ratio), and even more so with higher numbers of shares such as buying four puts to protect the unrealized profits in 300 shares (4-to-3).

Another consideration in these expanded ratios, besides the cost benefit in exchange for protection, is the degree of risk being hedged. The potential for losses in holdings of 400 shares is far more severe than for 100 shares, for example, so in those situations in which many 100-share lots are held, the insurance put may gain more importance and hedging value.

Long Puts to Hedge Covered Calls

Hedging long stock positions is perhaps the most obvious form of price protection based on puts. However, long puts can also be used to hedge risks associated with writing covered calls.

The covered call is widely considered to be a conservative strategy. The outcome is always profitable for the overall position if the proper call is utilized. If the call's time value diminishes enough, the short call is closed at a profit. If the call is exercised, you keep the premium and earn capital gains on the sales of stock (this requires, of course, that the strike price of the short call is higher than the original basis in stock). And if the short call expires worthless, the premium is 100 percent profit. But covered call writers can also lose if the value of the underlying falls lower than the net basis. (The net basis is equal to the original net cost of the stock reduced by the covered call premium.)

This risk is lower than the market risk of simply buying and holding stock. If the stock price declines, you end up with depreciated stock, worth less than you paid for it. So the covered call risk is lower because the span of risk is reduced by the call premium. This is not a risk specifically unique to writing covered calls, but a modification of the long stock market risk. Even so, the risk exists and especially so in highly volatile markets.

The risk can be mitigated using insurance puts as a hedge against market risk. When you buy a put to protect against the downside risk in the stock (market risk), holding a covered call at the same time benefits in two ways. First, the covered call reduces the net basis in long stock; and second, the premium you receive for selling the call may provide all or part of the premium you must pay to buy the insurance put.

> **Key Point:** Insurance puts should be considered as hedges against market risk; this is not the same as merely taking profits, although in a price decline that is what occurs.

This strategy eliminates risk in the stock and is called a *protective collar* (more commonly, it is simply called a *collar*). In the past, the short call and long put combination with 100 shares of long stock was also called a hedge wrapper, but this terminology is not often heard today. Most covered call writers analyze their positions by comparing overall income potential from the short call (plus dividends and capital gains). Adding the long put reduces this potential income, but it remains a sound strategy in two regards. First, it does eliminate the market risk of stock that exists even in a profitable covered call strategy. Second, the short call premium may be high enough to pay the long put premium, making the collar a no-cost strategy that provides complete elimination of extended market risk. As long as the put remains open, any drops in the stock below the put's strike will be offset by corresponding growth in the put's intrinsic value.

This collar can be entered at the time stock is purchased, not so much to profit from covered calls but to gain ownership of stock with no downside risk. The covered call provides cash to pay for the long put, and if the stock's value falls, the put can be sold at an offsetting profit or even exercised. Because it may take considerable time for price movement to develop, consider using LEAPS covered calls and long puts in creating a collar. This provides longer-term protection without substantially increasing exposure to call exercise; greater time value provides more current income and more room for deterioration in time value premium before expiration.

Returning to the example of McDonald's, owning 100 shares and creating a collar based on 60 options, you could use those expiring in five months based on timing starting in January (June options). In this case the 60 call was at 5.10 and the 60 put was at 6.20; so the cost to create a collar was 1.10 ($110), not bad to create five months of downside risk hedge. However, looking at the 23-month LEAPS options that expired two years later, the 60 call was worth 10.20 and the 60 put at 13.40. The net cost here was 3.20 ($320)—more cost but an additional 18 months of protection. For a cost of $320, you could eliminate all risk below approximately $56 per share (based on the price per share of $59.50 minus the net cost of the call and put of 3.20).

You can also move into a collar position in stages. For example, you might buy the stock and then buy a put upon price appreciation to protect paper profits. Then, if it appears that price is not going to retreat immediately, you sell a covered call to produce current income and to offset the cost of the put, perhaps even create a net credit. Any position involving multiple stock and position entry can occur at the same time or in parts. The result is the same, but many positions are created to prevent further losses, take advantage of price growth, or take a defensive position when the stock becomes increasingly volatile.

Collars can also be more complex than those illustrated using 100 shares of stock, one short call, and one long put. For example, imagine you own 600 shares of stock; you can open three separate collars involving two calls and two puts on one-third of the portfolio, even using different strike prices and expirations:

> 200 shares plus two short 65 calls and two short 60 puts
> 200 shares plus two short 60 calls and two short 60 puts
> 200 shares plus two short 55 calls and two short 55 puts

These positions would be likely to evolve over time as the stock's price moves in one direction or another. Movement creates the need to hedge against potential market risk, while the collar itself creates protection for little or no net cost. This approach is valuable when you have made a large commitment in shares of stock for the long term, but the market has turned bearish and extremely volatile. You do not want to sell shares, especially if their value has fallen, but you do need to hedge the risk. In this case, variations on the no-cost or low-cost collar enable you to eliminate risk without added costs, and without the need to close stock positions at the worst possible time.

The same argument favoring no-cost collars works just as well when markets are volatile to the upside. An appreciated stock can be subjected to a collar and create substantial downside protection along with current income. The covered call portion, if exercised, produces a desirable capital gain because the strike is far higher than original cost; and the premium received upon selling the covered calls provides funds to buy long puts, protecting against the possibility of a price decline.

> **Key Point:** A collar can be used to create a zero-cost strategy, while also providing complete protection from market risk.

The no-cost collar gives you the best of both worlds. A price rise may result in exercise of the short call, leading to a profitable disposition of stock along with call premium income and dividend. A decline in the stock price allows you to close out the short call at a profit, while using the long put to offset losses in the stock. Because risk is eliminated on the downside, a price decline is good news on both sides of the transaction. If the price does rebound, it suits your long-term strategy of holding stock. In this situation, the collar hedged the long stock position and completely eliminated market risk; and the premium income from the short call paid for the long put.

Risk Considerations: Types of Risks

The preceding chapter examined and explained the risks of taking up positions in options. However, anyone who invests or trades in the market faces a number of different risks beyond the best-known market risk (the risk that values will decline instead of increase). With options, market risk can occur in one of two ways:

1. *Long position risk* is experienced when you buy an option and face declining time value within a finite period until expiration. In fact, this is a considerable risk because 75 percent of all long options expire worthless. This makes the point that overcoming declining time value is a formidable challenge.

   At the same time, the long position risk is always limited. You can never lose more than the cost of the option. So if you buy an option for 0.75 ($75), the maximum loss is never more than $75; in this respect, market risk is attractive. In comparison, taking up a long position in stock can be far more expensive because stock prices may decline, eroding your position's value indefinitely.

2. *Short position risk* is more complex. An uncovered short position is considered high risk. The reason is that a stock's price can, in theory at least, move indefinitely higher or lower than the current market value. The uncovered short call is probably the highest-risk options strategy you can enter because, again in theory, a stock's value can rise indefinitely. Anyone who opens an uncovered short call has to acknowledge this risk; but the fact that 75 percent of options expire worthless also works for the call seller.

A covered call is probably the most conservative options strategy. In this situation, you own 100 shares for each option sold. In the event of exercise, your 100 shares are called away at the strike price. The covered call writer should select a strike price that will produce a profit in the sale of stock to ensure that no losses would occur if and when the short call is exercised. The outcomes are all profitable: If the call is exercised, you keep the call premium, earn a capital gain from the sale of stock, and also get dividends for the holding period of the stock. If the call's value declines, it can be closed with a closing purchase transaction, at a profit. And if it expires worthless, you still own 100 shares of stock and you are free to sell another covered call.

You cannot "cover" a short put in the same manner as you cover a short call. However, an uncovered short put is not as risky as the uncovered short call. While a stock's price can rise indefinitely, it cannot fall beyond zero. Many observe that the difference between the strike price of the short put and zero is the maximum risk. But in practical terms, the real maximum risk is the net difference between the put's strike price and tangible book value per share.

> **Key Point:** A short put cannot be covered like a short call; however, synthetic positions can result from advanced uses of short puts.

The following sections describe additional forms of risk options traders and, for that matter, all investors, face, beyond market value.

Inflation and Tax Risk

The features of inflation and taxes are widely understood, but they are usually considered as separate forms of risk. Inflation—rising prices or, in its opposite effect, loss of purchasing power—causes a deterioration of capital over time. For example, at the end of 2008, you needed $4 to equal the purchasing power of $1 in 1975, due to inflation.[1]

---

[1] Source: MeasuringWorth Web site at www.measuringworth.com/ppowerus/, purchasing power calculator

Inflation has been an invisible force in recent years because it has been quite low. Figure 2.1 summarizes the rate of CPI-U, or inflation among all urban consumers.

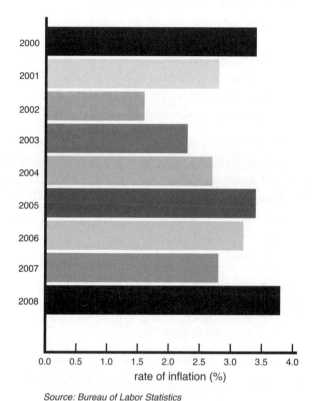

Source: Bureau of Labor Statistics

Figure 2.1   CPI-U rate of inflation, 2000-2008

This graph shows that inflation remained very low between 2000 and 2008. However, from 2009 forward, many economists predict rising inflation due to record-high federal budget deficits and spending. If this is the case, it means that investors will need to earn more return just to maintain the purchasing power of their capital.

The cost of inflation is an erosion cost. If your purchasing power falls net of inflation in the future, you lose true value. The previous illustration makes this point; if you had started an investment plan in 1975 and since then its overall value increased 400 percent, your purchasing power at the end of 2008—33 years later—would be identical to the original value in 1975. To maintain value with the inflation factor, you would need to earn an average of 4.25 percent each year, on a compounded basis.

Given the reality that most investors count profits at full dollar value, the effects of inflation are not widely appreciated. For example, if this year's inflation rate is 3 percent, a $1,000 profit is really worth only $970. When this effect is compounded over many years, the real impact of inflation is significant.

Even if you are aware of inflation and its eroding effect on your portfolio, you may not be aware of the tax risk. If your overall effective tax rate (the rate you pay on your taxable income) is 40 percent (assuming 33 percent federal and 7 percent state rates), you face an additional decline in net value of your investment profits. For example, that $1,000 profit declines to an after-tax value of only $600 after you pay your 40 percent tax.

Both inflation and taxes are serious matters because it means you need to earn *more* than you might think just to maintain your capital's value. When you look at the double effect of inflation and taxes, the true impact is troubling. In fact, you must earn an overall rate of 5 percent in your investment portfolio just to break even after inflation and taxes (based on assumed 3 percent inflation and 40 percent effective tax rate). For many moderate and conservative investors, this is not possible without increasing market risk exposure. This is the point at which options strategies can become very valuable as a hedge against the double impact of inflation and taxes.

> **Key Point:** Inflation and taxes are troubling risks separately. When combined, they present one of the most serious of all portfolio risks—because you can lose just by doing nothing.

To calculate your required breakeven rate of return after inflation and taxes, divide the assumed rate of inflation by your net after-tax income. The formula (with I indicating inflation and T your effective tax rate) is

$$I \div (100 - T)$$

Apply the previous example, using an assumed inflation rate of 3 percent and overall federal and state tax rate of 40 percent:

$$3\% \div (100 - 40) = 5\%$$

So if you earn 5 percent in this scenario, you break even. This means that you maintain your purchasing power, but you do not increase your post-inflation, post-tax value. Some investors need to redefine "profit" with this in mind. For some, just maintaining net purchasing power is a worthwhile goal. For others, the more traditionally understood concept of increased capital value is the goal. In this case, you need to begin using a more realistic understanding of "investment return." Given the fact that 5 percent is the breakeven, earning a return of 7 percent nets out at a gross of only 2 percent above the calculated breakeven. (Because the excess is also subject to inflation and taxes, the extra 2 percent is also reduced.) Consider this example comparing a 5 percent and a 7 percent return:

	5%	7%
Amount invested at beginning of year	$30,000	$30,000
Gross profit	$ 1,500	$ 2,100
Less taxes, 40%	– 600	– 840
After-inflation profit	$ 900	$ 1,260
Less inflation, 3% x $30,000	– 900	$ 900
Net after-tax profit and after-inflation	$ 0	$ 360
Year-end portfolio value, net	$30,000	$30,360
Net yield	0.0%	1.2%

This comparison demonstrates that although the 5 percent return produces no net gain, a 7 percent return produces not 2 percent more, but only 1.2 percent after inflation and taxes. So if the inflation and tax values apply to you and you earn 7 percent, the true net yield is really only 1.2 percent. The effects of inflation and taxes make it far more difficult to truly get ahead unless you are able to enhance profits with the use of options.

The breakeven rates at various rates of inflation and effective tax rates are shown in Table 2.2.

Table 2.2   Breakeven Rates

Effective Tax Rate	Inflation Rate					
	1%	2%	3%	4%	5%	6%
14%	1.2%	2.3%	3.5%	4.7%	5.8%	7.0%
16%	1.2	2.4	3.6	4.8	6.0	7.1
18%	1.2	2.4	3.7	4.9	6.1	7.3
20%	1.3	2.5	3.8	5.0	6.3	7.5
22%	1.3	2.6	3.8	5.1	6.4	7.
24%	1.3	2.6	3.9	5.3	6.6	7.9
26%	1.4	2.7	4.1	5.4	6.8	8.1
28%	1.4	2.8	4.2	5.6	6.9	8.3
30%	1.4	2.9	4.3	5.7	7.1	8.6
32%	1.5	2.9	4.4	5.9	7.4	8.8
34%	1.5	3.0	4.5	6.1	7.6	9.1
36%	1.6	3.1	4.7	6.3	7.8	9.4
38%	1.6	3.2	4.8	6.5	8.1	9.7
40%	1.7	3.3	5.0	6.7	8.3	10.0
42%	1.7	3.4	5.2	6.9	8.6	10.3
44%	1.8	3.6	5.4	7.1	8.9	10.7
46%	1.9	3.7	5.6	7.4	9.3	11.1
48%	1.9	3.8	5.8	7.7	9.6	11.5
50%	2.0	4.0	6.0	8.0	10.0	12.0
52%	2.1	4.2	6.3	8.3	10.4	12.5

Market Availability/Trade Disruption Risks

Some forms of risk are usually overlooked by investors, even though they are quite real and potentially damaging to your ability to take part in the market, trade in a timely manner, or deal with unexpected disruptions.

> **Key Point:** It is easy to overlook the possibility of a trade disruption; but if this does occur, short-term option positions could end up losing value entirely.

The simple availability of the market is assumed to be consistent. But there are going to be times when markets are not available. Each exchange has the right to curtail or stop trading on a specific stock (and its related options) or on the entire market. Catastrophic events such as the 9/11 attacks are the most severe causes for markets shutting down. Less severe market-wide causes may include automatic system failures or suspected viral attacks on the system. Markets will not be available on any issues when an exchange puts a circuit breaker into effect. This is a programmed trading halt that is used when values fall significantly in a single trading day (usually measured by the Dow Jones Industrial Average). For individual stocks, trading is halted when news is pending or released that may affect stock and option values, including rumors of mergers or other important events. A delayed opening or the outright halt of trading during the day is not unusual. In addition, trading may be halted due to severe trade imbalances in a single issue, when an excess of sellers over buyers (or vice versa) makes it impossible to continue an orderly market.

Portfolio and Knowledge/Experience Risks

Portfolio risk comes in many forms. For options traders, the most serious is found in a mix of stocks and options that is not going to achieve your investment goals. For example, if you sell shares of stock as soon as they become profitable, you dispose of the stronger issues, while leaving under-performers in place. Ultimately, you end up with a portfolio whose overall value is lower than your basis. One solution to this problem is to buy puts when stock values have risen. This costs money but, if the stock price declines, the put will gain value and offset any paper losses (or, more accurate, loss of paper profits). Options are effective for creating short-term profits without needing to dispose of shares you would prefer to keep for the long term.

Options traders also have to contend with knowledge risk. Brokers are required to ask every options trader to complete a trading application form. This form asks you to disclose your knowledge in options. If the brokerage firm believes that your knowledge is limited, the firm will allow you to trade only the most basic of strategies, found in one of several trading levels. In practical application, the amount of capital in your trading account also determines to some degree the level at which your broker will allow you to trade.

> **Key Point:** Knowledge risk—or, more accurately, lack of knowledge risk— can lead to trouble. Many options traders lose money because they simply have not learned how transactions can end up.

The lowest trading level is usually limited to long positions in calls and puts. As the levels advance, more complex and higher-risk strategies will be allowed. At the highest level, you are allowed to take either long or short positions and in advanced strategies and combinations. Even so, margin limits are going to apply to all open positions. You will be required to have on deposit an adequate level of securities and cash to cover any exercised options positions. This naturally limits the range of options positions you can open at any given time. The maximum margin leverage you are going to be allowed is 50 percent under Federal Reserve Regulation T (see www.federalreserve.gov).

Diversification and Asset Allocation Risk

Most people understand the concept of diversification; however, accomplishing it is not as easy as many believe. Simply putting money into several different stocks does not necessarily diversify a portfolio.

Two dangers have to be contended with in this regard: over- and under-diversification. The latter is well understood; clearly, putting too high a portion of your capital into a single stock is taking a great risk. But diversifying too extensively is also a risk because the overall return will approach only the average of the entire set. In this situation, excelling and beating the market is made more difficult by the extent of diversification.

You achieve diversification in several ways. They include

- Investing in more than one stock.
- Selecting stocks in industries subject to dissimilar market, economic, and cyclical influences.
- Spreading capital among different products (stocks, debt securities, real estate, and options, for example).
- Relying on others to diversify your portfolio (investing in mutual funds or exchange-traded funds instead of in individual stocks).
- Diversifying by levels of risk (this is where options are quite useful; for example, you may take higher risks with options positions combined with relatively lower risks in long stock positions; buying puts to provide insurance for stock paper profits also diversifies risk exposure).

Asset allocation is a form of broad diversification, in which the overall portfolio is invested by formula into different product areas. Most popular among these are stocks, debt securities, money markets, and real estate. The danger in allocation is that it is determined by percentage based on changing market conditions, but this could mean that your portfolio gets unbalanced rather than the objective of spreading risks by balancing the markets. The risk is further augmented when the allocation method is not rational. For example, should you consider the equity in your home as part of an allocated portfolio, or should that be left out of the mix? If you had a large allocation percentage in real estate from late 2007 until mid-2009, you would have probably lost value in your overall portfolio, at least partially due to unintentional overloading of real estate. So allocation may be a sound technique for spreading risks, but current market conditions should determine the degree of allocation rather than an assumed or fixed percentage breakdown.

Leverage Risk

The common methods of investing can be broken down into two types: equity and debt. The equity market includes any ownership position in stocks or mutual fund shares, real estate, and other tangible assets. Debt includes bonds, income mutual fund shares, and the money market. A third but often overlooked category is leverage.

> **Key Point:** Whenever you leverage your capital to increase your exposure to profit opportunities, you also increase your exposure to the chances of loss. The two cannot be separated.

When you buy an option, you spend a fraction of the cost for 100 shares of the underlying stock, but you control those 100 shares just as if you had purchased them. By exercising your option, you can buy (through a call) or sell (through a put) 100 shares even though your exposure to risk is far more limited than through full purchase.

Leverage risk comes up when you use margin accounts to invest, doubling your investment capital but committing yourself to a repayment obligation even if your investments lose value. And you have to pay interest on borrowed money as well. The cash flow problems of leverage arise when you are required to make periodic repayments whether your investments are profitable or not. Using borrowed funds to speculate in the market is very high-risk and beyond the risk tolerance levels for many people. However, options strategies may approximate the same opportunities for only a fraction of the risk; this makes options very attractive to those interested in speculating in the market.

Options can also be used as a form of leverage in strategies such as swing trading. This allows you to use limited capital more efficiently by broadening your exposure; it also limits risk to your long position costs rather than needing to go short at the top of a price swing. Options solve many of these problems, and swing traders can use calls and puts (both in long positions) as an alternative to switching between long and short positions in shares of stock.

Liquidity Risk (Lost Opportunity Risk)

There are many definitions of *liquidity*. It refers to working capital, market conditions, and risk. Risk-based liquidity is simply having cash and credit available to invest when opportunities arise. But if you are fully invested, you are likely to miss out on opportunities when they emerge. They can take several forms.

> **Key Point:** Being fully invested means keeping your money at work; it could also mean you are not able to move into a position when an opportunity presents itself.

For example, if you are fully invested and your positions include short options, you may want to close out positions when values decline. But this is possible only if you have the funds on hand. Otherwise, you are forced to miss the opportunity, and as a consequence you could end up with a loss instead of a gain.

Options can be used to solve liquidity-based problems as well. For example, you are nearly fully invested, but you would like to buy 100 shares of a stock that is currently available at a bargain price. Rather than having to buy 100 shares, you can buy a call (or sell a put) as a form of contingent or deferred purchase. In this way, a leveraged position overcomes liquidity problems. So liquidity can be either a risk or the basis for a strategy in certain market conditions, specifically when markets are overbought or oversold and you anticipate a reversal.

Goal-based Risks

Another risk not often discussed is the potential of losing sight of well-expressed, specific goals. For example, if your goal is to seek current income through higher-than-average dividends, you might wander from this purpose by picking stocks with high option values as part of a combination strategy. This may produce greater income than the dividend-based idea, but it also ties up capital and does away with flexibility. If part of the long-term plan was to reinvest dividends in additional partial shares (creating a compound dividend return), the alternative of seeking higher-than-average option income could produce greater yield, but the long-term is an unknown. This switch in strategies also defeats the desirable compounding effect of reinvestment.

Error Risks

One final type of risk is found in simple errors. Options traders, like everyone else, make mistakes. But with options, these mistakes can be potentially very expensive. For example, entering a sell order when you intended to enter a buy order exposes you to far greater risk levels than intended, and by the time the error is discovered you may have already incurred big losses. Another mistake is missing an expiration date and discovering—too late—that a position you intended to close has been exercised or expired worthless.

In the options market, making a simple mistake can have high financial consequences. For this reason alone, the error risk has to be diligently managed and guarded against, through double-checking and verification steps at the time of order entry.

In the next chapter, the concept of the insurance put is examined in detail. This strategy allows you to take profits on appreciated stock, but without needing to sell the stock.

3

PROFIT-TAKING WITHOUT SELLING STOCK: AN ELEGANT SOLUTION

The dilemma every stockholder faces is timing. When should you take profits? Does it even make sense to sell appreciated stock given the positive attributes of the company (such as high dividends, strong fundamentals, excellent growth forecasts)? The temptation to take profits when they are earned can be very enticing.

This situation occurs when, for a variety of reasons, stock values jump and reach new highs, for reasons you cannot identify. Or even if you know the reasons, the extent of the price increase is not justified. For example, if a company beats earnings estimates for a quarter by one penny and the stock jumps 10 percent, does it make sense? You know that chances are high the price is going to retreat in coming trading sessions. So you could sell stock now and take profits and then repurchase shares when the price falls back. However, in some instances the stock price continues to rise, meaning a premature disposal of a good stock ends up a big mistake. But there is a solution: puts.

The Insurance Put

The preceding chapter explained insurance puts and their variations. To continue this discussion, this chapter compares insurance puts to simply holding stock, describes how the collar is created, and explains how entering an advanced strategy at the wrong time can have serious tax consequences.

In the basic insurance put strategy, you can take profits without selling stock. For every 100 shares you own, you buy one put. However, this is a simplified explanation of the strategy; there is more involved. Picking the most appropriate put to protect paper profits requires careful comparisons among several available puts. The premium you pay for this insurance put accomplishes two goals. First, it allows you to continue holding onto your stock; and second, it provides profits if and when the stock price declines. As the price declines, the intrinsic value of your put rises point for point with the loss in the stock.

> **Key Point:** Insurance puts provide not only profits, but elimination of downside market risk.

If you buy a put with excessive time value premium, you reduce the chances that the insurance put will serve its intended purpose. So you need a reasonable amount of time before expiration, but at a relatively controlled level of cost. Without this analysis, you may end up seeing little offset between dwindling paper profits and growth put value because extrinsic value will offset intrinsic value. In that case, the insurance put could be an expensive mistake. The solution is to look at all the alternatives and pick the option that is going to work best. This sometimes means settling for partial protection and leaving some level of paper profits at risk.

What if you buy an insurance put but the stock continues to rise in value? There are instances when sudden rise in a stock's price is not a momentary aberration but the beginning of a price breakout to the upside. In this case, the long put is going to lose value and eventually expire worthless. However, because you continue to own 100 shares of stock for each put, you profit from gains in the stock price. Given the alternative—selling stock to take profits and losing out on further gains—the relatively small price of buying the insurance put is worth the risk.

An alternative strategy overcomes the problem of lost put premium, but it offsets one problem with another. Writing a covered call also enables you to take paper profits without selling stock. In this strategy, you sell one call per 100 shares held. If the stock price falls, the short call also loses value, offsetting all or part of the paper loss in stock. This is quite a conservative strategy because, if you pick a call that will produce a gain in the stock if exercised, you will profit in almost every outcome (the one exception occurs when the stock price declines substantially; however, in that event, holding the shares without any option strategies will produce the same negative outcome). As you will see later in this chapter, your choices are not limited to covered calls or insurance puts; combining these can provide protection and short-term income.

The covered call is advantageous because you are paid the premium; in the event the stock value declines, you can easily close the position at a profit or allow the short call to expire worthless. However, if the stock price continues to rise, you face the chance of exercise. In this case, your stock is called away at the strike price. Compared to simply taking your profits by selling stock, the covered call is far more profitable. Upon exercise, you earn a capital gain on the stock; the option premium is 100 percent profit; and you continue to earn dividends as long as the stock is yours.

> **Key Point:** Covered call writing makes sense only if the strike is higher than your basis in the stock; this creates profits from three sources: call premium, dividends, and capital gains.

Exercise can be avoided in the short call by rolling forward. In this exercise-avoidance strategy, you buy to close the original short call position and replace it with another call expiring later. This defers exercise and produces additional cash income. (It does not insure against early exercise, but it reduces the odds.) Ideally, a forward roll can also replace the current call's strike price with a strike one increment higher. This not only makes exercise more remote, but in the event of ultimate exercise, also produces higher profits in the sale of exercised stock. A word of caution, however: In replacing an existing call with one of the same strike price and a later exercise, you could change the status of long-term capital gains on stock. If the new call falls into the realm on an unqualified covered call, tax rules specify that you may lose long-term gains status. This means that if and when exercised, your stock would be fully taxed at ordinary rates. This occurs because the period leading up to long-term treatment is suspended while you have an open position in an unqualified covered call (defined as a call more than one strike increment in the money at most price levels).

> **Valuable Resource:** Learn more about qualified and unqualified covered calls by downloading the free IRS Publication 550, at www.irs.gov/publications/p550/ch04.html.

For many stock investors who (a) want to hold onto shares for the long term and (b) are not willing to risk exercise through covered calls, the relatively low cost of the insurance put is a sensible alternative. It solves the problem of profit-taking by setting up a situation providing for keeping shares, while protecting the paper losses through the long put. It also overcomes the problems of covered call writing, specifically the risk of having shares called away. Even if exercise produces a profit, you may still prefer to hold onto shares as long-term value investments.

Insurance put costs vary with the time until expiration and the proximity between the current value of shares and the put's strike. The lower the cost, the less effective the insurance. You are constantly struggling with the exchange between three attributes: time to expiration, proximity of strike to current share price, and cost.

Picking the Best Long Put: Time, Proximity, and Cost

To maximize the advantages of the put insurance strategy but without incurring excessive cost, you need to balance the three ingredients of time to expiration, proximity of the put to the current stock strike to price, and cost. In the preceding chapter, examples showed the effect of the insurance put; the following explanation takes this a step beyond, showing you how to select the best insurance put based on the circumstances in play.

To select the most appropriate put for insurance of your paper profits,
you need to study a range of available puts and compare the three
attributes. For example, you own 100 shares of SPDR Gold Trust, which
you bought at $87 per share. The price recently spiked to $92 per share
and has been volatile between $88 and $94. You are considering buying
a put to protect paper profits. You review strikes between 84 and 90,
and expiring in two, three, and six months. When shares of SPDR Gold
Trust Shares (GLD) were at $91.99 (a March time frame), available puts
ranged from 84 to 90 as shown in Table 3.1.

Table 3.1   Gold Trust (GLD)

Strike	Put Bid Prices at the Close		
Price	May Puts	Jun Puts	Sep Puts
84	2.60	3.70	6.20
85	2.95	4.10	6.70
86	3.30	4.50	7.10
87	3.70	4.90	7.60
88	4.10	5.40	8.10
89	4.60	5.90	8.70
90	5.00	6.40	9.20

The three attributes you need to review—time to expiration, proximity
of the put to the current stock strike to price, and cost—are used to
decide which put to buy for insurance of the appreciated share price.

Expiration: The May puts provide only two months of protection, but given the volatility of GLD, this could be adequate. It depends on your plans. If you want to sell these shares within two months, the May put is appropriate. If you want to hold shares longer, consider the June or September puts. Your original basis was $87 per share; if you buy a 90 put for 5 ($500), you end up with net protection at the $85-per-share level. (The 90 put, if exercised, allows you to sell shares three points above your basis of 87, but the cost is five points. Thus, your net protection level—worst case—is $85 per share ($90 − $87 = $3 profit) offset by put cost of $5 (loss = $2 per share).

Proximity: Current value of the stock at this point was $91.99 per share, or nearly five points above your original basis. There are two ways to ensure taking this profit: selling shares now or buying one of several puts. The 90 puts provide the greatest protection but cost more than strikes further away. Picking the appropriate proximity relies on how much protection you want and how much of your paper profits you want to protect.

Cost: The dilemma for any long options trader is the offset between time value and cost. In this example, cost varies on a predictable scale. The more out of the money and the closer expiration, the cheaper the put. So it is a balancing act to pick an option that (a) addresses the need and (b) is not overly expensive. One advantage of puts close to expiration is that they contain very little time value premium. For example, the May 90 is 4.20 lower than the equivalent September 90. Because all these premium levels represent nonintrinsic value, the comparison tells the whole story. You pay for more time; so if your position in the stock is worth protecting, you will have to pay for that protection. In the event the stock price declines, the long put creates a floor and limits your maximum loss. If the price rises, your profit is reduced by the premium for the put. For example, if you paid 5 for a May 90 put, at the point where the underlying is worth $92 per share, you would be at breakeven: $92 − 87 = $5. This does not include the transaction costs to open and to close any position, so the real breakeven may be up to one-half point higher.

Another consideration in the evaluation of an insurance put is the dividend you earn on the underlying. For example, if you owned shares of

3M (MMM) early in 2009, your dividend yield was 4.8 percent (based on price of $43). This is a considerable yield, and one way to look at it is that the dividend reduces the cost of the insurance put. This is one of several factors to include in the equation, making the overall cost-versus-benefit analysis more clear. It is always the case that dividend yield should be considered in the overall analysis of returns from stock and option strategies; in this application, you may consider dividends as a discount to the cost of an insurance put.

Buying Puts Versus Short-selling Stock

If you believe a stock is going to fall in value, puts play a vital role in managing your portfolio. However, options are relatively new on the scene and are becoming increasingly popular for reducing losses in long stock positions. Conversely, a more traditional strategy is selling stock short. Compared to buying long puts, this is a very risky strategy that also costs more (due to interest you have to pay your broker).

> **Key Point:** The practice known as short selling does not make sense when compared to long puts; these are less expensive and contain much less risk.

Short selling stock involves the following steps:

1. Your broker buys the shares for you (or uses shares in his or her own account).

2. You "borrow" the shares from your broker to sell them short.

3. When you sell the shares, proceeds are credited to your account.

4. The transaction is closed when you cover the position with a buy order. At that point, you are no longer short. If the stock price fell, you make a profit because you buy to close at a lower price than your sale price. If the stock price rose, you have a loss from two sources. First, you lose in the net difference between sale and buy prices. Second, you lose the interest you paid to the broker for the borrowed shares.

The purpose of selling short has always been to profit after a stock's price falls. Clearly, this is an uncovered risk; if the stock price rises, the short seller loses money and that loss could potentially be significant. In comparison, buying a long put involves far less cost and less risk. You can never lose more than the premium cost of the put; and if the stock price does fall, the decline is matched point for point in intrinsic value of your long put.

Returning to the GLD example: Current value rounded up to about $92 per share. You can sell the stock short at $92 anticipating a price decline. Your broker loans 100 shares to you, and upon sale, the proceeds are deposited into your account. As an alternative you can sell a May 90 put for 5 ($500). Compare the outcome at various price levels as shown in Table 3.2.

Table 3.2 Comparing Short Selling to Long Puts

Description of Change in Stock Price	Selling Short	Buying a 90 Put
The stock price falls to $86 per share.	The profit at this point is $400.	The loss at this point is $100 (premium 5 minus price change 4).
The stock price falls to $76 per share.	The profit at this point is $1,400.	The profit at this point is $900 (14 points of intrinsic value minus 5).
The stock price rises to $90 per share.	The loss at this point is $400.	The loss at this point is fixed at $500.
The stock price rises to $100 per share.	The loss at this point is $1,400.	The loss at this point is fixed at $500.

If selling short turns out to be a smart move, the profit is going to be greater than buying the insurance put. The difference is equal to the premium cost of the put. Yet, when you consider not only the dollar amount but the yield as well, the picture is quite different. For example, if GLD fell to $76 per share, the short stock profit is $1,400, but the amount at risk was $9,200; so this is a net yield of 15.2 percent ($1,400 ÷ $9,200). The same price decline with a long put produces a profit of

$900. The original cost was $500, so the profit in this instance would be 180 percent ($900 ÷ $500).

> **Key Point:** Always compare outcomes in all possible situations to determine relative pros and cons of a strategy. Short selling stock versus buying puts is a good example of why this is important.

It is not only the yield that makes long puts more desirable than selling stock short. It is also the level of risk. In selling short, you expose yourself to considerably higher risks. If the stock price rises (potentially quite high), the loss grows point for point with the higher stock price. However, the maximum loss for the long put is always fixed at your premium cost.

Rolling into Spreads to Offset Put Losses

The best-known version of "rolling forward" involves short option positions, but a variation also helps long put owners to offset losses by creating a new position through the forward roll.

In the short call roll, a call seller replaces one short call with a later-expiring call, either at the same strike or at a higher strike. This accomplishes several goals. First, it avoids impending exercise. Second, it creates additional income due to time value. Third, if the new strike is higher than the one it replaces, it builds in additional profits if and when the short position is exercised.

In the short put roll, the idea is the same, but the direction is different. A put seller replaces one short put with a later-expiring put, either at the same strike or at a *lower* strike. This accomplishes the same goals as those of the short call roll.

The same idea is useful when you have purchased a long put and it has lost value, due to a declining time value, lack of intrinsic value build-up, or both. The offset is created by converting the solitary long spread. This can either reduce a loss or limit the profit, but it is preferable to losing all the premium invested in the long put. For example, assume

---

you own 100 shares of stock you bought at $87 per share, and you also purchased a long put at 5 ($500) when the underlying stock was at $92. Since then the stock has risen to $95 per share and your put's value has fallen to 2 ($200). The 95 put at this time is worth 3 ($300). At this point, the spread strategy has two segments. First, sell two of the 90 puts, creating a credit of $400, and buy one 95 put for 6 ($300). The net credit in this transaction is $100 ($400 − $300). This reduces your original $500 premium to $400.

This transaction eliminates the original long position and replaces it with a short, and adds a new long put at a higher strike. The advantage to this position is twofold. First, if you consider the higher put as a form of replacement insurance, it provides that insurance at a higher strike, which as a holder of long stock is a definite advantage (it is worth $500 in the event of a price decline). Second, while reducing your net investment basis in the put positions, there is no greater risk. If the stock's value declines, the long 95 and the short 90 will both increase in value to the same degree below the lower strike of 90 because both will be in the money. However, if the stock's value continues to rise, you have merely replaced one insurance put with another, and the overall investment netting out at $400 is offset by higher value in the underlying.

> **Key Point:** Rolling forward is a great strategy to avoid exercise, create additional income, and move the strike increment into a more profitable range.

Because one long put has been replaced with another at a higher strike, this is one form of rolling forward. Unlike the roll for a short put, where an existing strike is merely extended or replaced with a later-expiring put with a *lower* strike, the long put is rolled forward to a higher-strike, later-expiring long put. The additional cost of the higher-strike long put is offset (and in this case by a $100 credit) by the short puts at the lower strikes.

Another variation of this concept—converting a long put—is the calendar spread strategy. In this situation, assuming the same set of facts as in the preceding example, you sell a put at the same strike but expiring sooner. This accomplishes a net credit, reducing the cost of the original insurance put. Because the stock's price has risen, the chances of exercise are greatly reduced, and selling a sooner-expiring put creates a credit, thus reducing the cost of the original long put. If the stock were to continue rising, both puts expire worthless and the short put's premium is converted to profit, whereas the long put is a total loss.

The calendar spread is a no-loss strategy. If the stock rises, the additional credit is yours to keep. If the stock's price declines, any increase in the short put's value is offset by a corresponding in-the-money increase in the later-expiring long put. Whenever the long position has more time to go to expiration, the risk in the short position at the same strike is entirely offset.

This idea can be expanded to even more complex strategies. Given the need for a stock to decline substantially to go in the money, the calendar spread can be converted to a ratio calendar spread. For example, if you sell two intermediate puts as an offset to the existing long position, you double the credit you receive in exchange for greater risk. The net risk is limited to one put. Of the two short positions, one is offset by the later-expiring put, and the other is completely exposed. But how much risk is involved in this? The actual risk, in fact, is the strike price of the put minus the credit received for selling the two puts.

> **Key Point:** The true market risk in a calendar spread is not as severe as it might seem at first glance.

In the event the stock's value rises, both of the short puts are profitable. If the stock's price falls, you can take one of three actions:

1. *Close one of the short puts.* The easiest action is to close one of the two short puts. If time value has declined since the positions were opened, it is likely that you can create a small profit in the transaction, assuming that you take action before the put moves in the money. Once intrinsic value begins to accumulate, you would only be able to close at a loss.

2. *Roll forward and down to avoid exercise.* The second approach to avoid exercise is to close one or both of the short puts with a closing purchase transaction and replace with later-expiring puts. These may be at the same strike or at a lower strike. The roll forward to a later-expiring strike will create yet another net

credit. Rolling to a lower strike may create a small debit or, in some cases (depending on how much more time is involved), you may create a credit while exchanging for a lower strike.

3. *Accept exercise of the second short put.* If you are willing to acquire more shares of the underlying at the strike, simply letting it get exercised is one available way to go. This is especially advantageous when the net difference between the strike price and current market value is at or below the net profit of the short puts. For example, if you net out at three points, but the stock is only two points below the put strike, you will be ahead by the difference of one point ($100) by just letting exercise occur. Even if you are at breakeven or at a small loss in the exercise scenario, this can be offset through additional option-based action. For example, you can write covered calls against your long shares to further improve short-term profits while reducing the net basis in the underlying.

Buying Puts to Protect Covered Call Positions

Covered call writing generally is viewed as a low-risk transaction. This is true because all outcomes are either profitable or better than simply owning stock. Puts can play a role in reducing the limited risk that is involved.

In the covered call position, you own 100 shares of stock and sell one call. If the stock rises in value, the call may be exercised and the stock called away at the strike price. Thus, you would lose the appreciated value of stock that you could have had without selling the call. Even so, covered call writers exchange that lost opportunity for the certainty of covered call profits. As long as the exercise price is higher than the original basis in stock, four outcomes are possible:

1. The call value declines and is sold at a profit.

2. The call value declines and expires worthless.

3. The call value increases after it moves in the money and is exercised. (Exercise can be deferred or avoided with a roll forward or roll forward and up.)

4. Stock value falls significantly. In this outcome the covered call expires worthless, but stock has also lost value. In comparison to simply owning shares, the covered call mitigates the paper loss, but not always enough to offset it completely.

> **Key Point:** When you have many possible outcomes, always assume the worst one will occur, and then look for ways to reduce or eliminate that risk.

In the fourth outcome, a conservative investor may worry about potential losses from committing stock via a covered call. Thus, a bailout is not practical because selling the stock will leave an uncovered call, greatly increasing the market risk. Puts offer a solution to this problem. In the preceding chapter, some collar examples and strategies were introduced; following is a detailed examination of the outcome in which a collar is designed to completely eliminate market risk, in exchange for lower profit potential.

A collar combines a covered call with a long put, which eliminates virtually all market risk for as long as the put remains open. This is the case as long as (1) the call's strike is higher than the original basis in stock so that in the event of exercise, the stock will be called away at a profit, (2) the short call premium is higher than the long put premium, and (3) you do not close any of the portions of this position early, which greatly increases the risk (especially if the stock is sold, leaving the short call uncovered).

For example, assume that Apple Computer (AAPL) is $85.30. If you had originally purchased 100 shares at $83 and you were concerned about price volatility, you could sell a covered call as one plan; or you could sell a call and buy a put to provide downside protection. This course creates far less profit, but it is one alternative if you are concerned with market volatility. A summary of available calls and puts assuming a March timeline is provided in Table 3.3.

Table 3.3 Apple Computer (AAPL) (March Timeline)

Strike Price	Call Bid Prices at the Close			Put Bid Prices at the Close		
	Apr Calls	Jul Calls	Oct Calls	Apr Puts	Jul Puts	Oct Puts
80	9.75	14.60	17.75	4.35	9.00	*11.95*
85	6.85	11.90	*15.15*	6.45	11.30	14.35
90	4.55	9.55	12.85	9.10	13.90	17.00

Your original basis in this stock was $83, but you are concerned that prices could fall below that level. The usual benefit of selling a covered call is that it discounts the basis. For example, you could sell an April 85 call and receive 6.85 ($685). This exposes you for one month but yields 8.3 percent based on your purchase price of $83 per share ($685 ÷ $8,300). Because this exposure maximum is only one month, the annualized return is 99.6 percent (one month multiplied by 12). This does not imply that you can always earn returns close to 100 percent on covered calls, but it does provide a good means for comparison between various outcomes. If the call is exercised, you keep the $685 and also earn $200 in capital gains on sale of the stock.

> **Key Point:** Most covered call examples focus on the profitable outcomes, but if the stock declines substantially, you also need to identify a method for mitigating the stock loss.

As an alternative, you could also sell a July 85 call for 11.90. This is a four-month return of 14.3 percent (annualized 42.9 percent). Or you could sell a covered October 85 call for 15.15, which is a seven-month return of 18.3 percent (annualized calculation: 18.3 ÷ 7 × 12 = 31.4 percent). The longer you extend the covered call's period, the higher the dollar amount but the lower the annualized yield.

As attractive as the covered call is for double-digit returns, you might hesitate to enter into this position out of fear of market volatility in the stock. In fact, that fear alone may even prevent you from buying shares of stock. The collar, however, can produce cash income while eliminating most of the market risk. For example, note in Table 3.3 that one call and one put were highlighted. The October 85 call was worth 15.15 and the October 80 put was worth 11.95.

If you had bought 100 shares at 83 and then sold the October 85 call and bought the October 80 put, you would have created a collar. The net credit on the two options was 3.20, or $320. The outcomes based on values at expiration (calculating only intrinsic value of the options) at various levels of stock price are summarized in Table 3.4.

Table 3.4   Outcome of the Collar

Stock Price	Stock Profit or Loss	Short October 85 Call	Long October 80 Put	Total Profit or Loss
$75	$–800	$1,515	– 695	$ 20
76	–700	1,515	– 795	20
77	–600	1,515	– 895	20
78	–500	1,515	– 995	20
79	–400	1,515	–1,095	20
80	–300	1,515	–1,195	20
81	–200	1,515	–1,195	120
82	–100	1,515	–1,195	220
83	0	1,515	–1,195	320
84	100	1,515	–1,195	420
85	200	1,515	–1,195	520
86	300	1,415	–1,195	520
87	400	1,315	–1,195	520
88	500	1,215	–1,195	520
89	600	1,115	–1,195	520
90	700	1,015	–1,195	520

In this example, risk has been removed completely (but without considering transaction costs). The *worst* outcome occurs when the stock closes at or below $80 per share. In this situation, you face the maximum cost for the cost coupled with a three-point decline in the stock, offset by the entire call premium. These outcomes all assume that the options will be closed on the day of expiration. The maximum profit is fixed at $20 if the stock falls below $80 per share, and at $520 if the stock rises above $84 per share. If the short call is exercised, the net outcome remains the same because the entire call premium is yours to keep.

> **Key Point:** Whether options in a collar are closed on the day of expiration, or in-the-money portions of the position are exercised, the strategy fixed profits by eliminating downside market risk.

For example, if the stock closed at $90 per share, stock would be called away at $85, but you would retain the call premium:

Stock profit	$ 200
Short call profit	1,515
Total	$1,715

This outcome is identical to the outcome resulting from the sale of the call on the day of expiration.

However, a strategy such as this clearly limits your maximum profit, at least during the period that the collar remains open. At the close of the position, you are free to enter a subsequent one, assuming you wish to continue owning the stock. It is an appropriate strategy only if you are so worried about the risk of a decline in the stock's value that you are willing to give up larger profits from selling a call. If you simply held 100 shares and sold the October 85 call, this would discount your basis by 15.15 points:

Original basis	$ 8,300
Less: call premium	−1,515
Net basis	$ 6,785

With this discount in mind, you could tolerate a considerable decline in the stock's market value before you would experience a net loss. So in comparing the covered call strategy to the collar, you need to evaluate the differences in net return, as well as the value of eliminating market risk.

Tax Problems with Long Puts

The tax rules for options trading contain a few oddities, so before entering collars and other advanced strategies, you need to consult with your tax expert. Otherwise, you might discover that current-year losses may not be deductible or that what you thought was a long-term capital gain has reverted to short-term.

If you own stock purchased far enough in the past to already qualify for long-term gains treatment and you then buy a put, there is no effect on the capital gains status or deductibility of losses. However, if (1) you buy shares and at the same time buy a put or (2) own shares not yet qualified for long-term treatment, the story is more complicated. If you have held stock for less than the period required to qualify for long-term capital gains (one year), the holding period is returned to zero. This means you have no accumulated time toward the long-term mark. In addition, you cannot begin the count again until the put has been closed.

> **Key Point:** Be careful when you buy puts if you also own stock. Unless you have already qualified for long-term gains treatment, you could lose that right and be required to start counting all over again.

For example, if you bought stock 11 months ago and it has appreciated in value, buying a put today wipes out the 11 months. You cannot begin the count again until the put is sold or closed. So if you sell stock at any time before a new 12-month period has begun after the put is closed, you will be taxed at ordinary, short-term rates.

This does not affect the insurance put situation when stock has been held for a long enough period to already qualify for a lower tax rate due to long-term gains rules. In that scenario, you buy stock, it appreciates, and then you buy a put to protect your paper profits. In this case, the stock status is not changed, and the put is not *married* to the stock for tax purposes.

Even though tax rules inhibit many tax planning situations, this does not mean that combined strategies are entirely off the table. Several situations make you immune to the negative tax consequences. Two, in particular, are

1. When you are trading in a qualified tax-sheltered plan. In this kind of account, no income is taxed until funds are removed, and all income is taxed at ordinary rates. Thus, the consequences of losing long-term gains status do not apply.

2. When you have large carryover losses. You are allowed to deduct only up to $3,000 per year in investment losses; however, after the huge market declines of 2008 and 2009, many people were left with large carryover losses that might never be completely used up. The only advantage to this is that the losses can be used to offset future gains, including short-term gains resulting from options strategies.

> **Key Point:** If you have large carryover losses, you can afford to lose long-term status in your positions because you can absorb current profits in the loss carryover.

The many strategies aimed at insuring profits are flexible and involve combinations of long and short puts and the use of calls. In later chapters, descriptions of the uses of spreads, straddles, and ratio combinations move this discussion into more advanced areas. By hedging positions, you can use puts to not only manage your portfolio, but to create additional profits, not necessarily with added market risk.

In addition to protecting paper profits with the use of long puts, you can also trade short-term gains through swing trading. Although this activity is most often described using shares of stock, there are many advantages—and lower—risks involved when you swing trade with options. And this is one situation in which options expiring very soon are preferable over longer-term options with greater time value. The next chapter explains swing trading as an options strategy and demonstrates how puts are used to eliminate risks.

4

SWING TRADING WITH PUTS: LONG AND SHORT OR COMBINED WITH CALLS

T he strategy called *swing trading* is so named because it involves profiting from the very short-term price swings in a stock. A swing trader focuses on the stock rather than on the company, and in highly volatile markets, this approach to trading can be quite effective.

This chapter describes the basic swing trading theory and demonstrates how to recognize the important price patterns that signal entry and exit points from positions. However, beyond this, the chapter also shows how options can play a part in swing trading. The majority of swing trading activity takes place using long and short stock positions. By replacing shares of stock with options, you gain several advantages. They include

1. *Leverage of capital.* One big problem in the traditional swing trading system is that capital is invariably limited. You can swing trade only to the extent that your portfolio allows; this means you can trade only a finite number of shares in any one company, and also that you have to limit swing trading to a very small number of companies (even if you would like to expand this activity to many more stocks).

2. *Reduced risk on the sell side.* Swing traders who believe a stock's price is at the high end of the price swing traditionally sell stock short to enter a position. (If they have previously bought shares at the bottom of the swing, this would also signal a sell.) Shorting stock is a high-risk strategy; if the stock's price rises instead of falls, the short position can be an expensive timing mistake. For this reason, many swing traders limit their strategy to buying at the bottom and then closing the position at the top. So half of the profit potential is passed up.

   This problem is overcome with the use of options. Anyone who is not willing to sell short can use long puts as an alternative. The risk is always limited to the premium of the put, but the exposure to profit potential is identical to shorting stock. Because a put is far cheaper than selling short 100 shares, the return percentage is also substantially greater.

3. *Reduced risk overall, using long options.* The risks of using shares to swing trade, whether long or short, involve timing. Even on the long side, you face risk when using stock. Going long at the bottom of a swing may be profitable, but if the stock continues to fall, this will end up in a loss. In the alternative, using calls and puts in place of stock limits your risk to the premium you pay.

4. *Greater flexibility.* When you swing trade using stock, you really have only two choices. You can be either long (a buyer) or short (a seller). However, when you use options, your range of strategic choices is expanded. The most obvious and practical strategy is to use long calls at the bottom of the swing and long puts at the top. You also limit your approach to using long and short puts, long and short calls, or a combination of short calls and short puts. Depending on market conditions and your risk tolerance level, any of these strategies presents interesting variations on the basic idea of swing trading.

> **Key Point:** Using options to swing trade is more advantageous than using shares of stock because of leverage, lower risk, and greater flexibility.

Basics of Swing Trading

The whole idea of swing trading is based on the recognition of short-term trends. Swing traders define an *uptrend* as three or more consecutive days (or shorter time increments) in which two things occur. First, the closing price is higher than the previous day's closing price; and second, the day's lowest price is higher than the previous day's closing price. This pattern is shown in Figure 4.1.

Yahoo chart

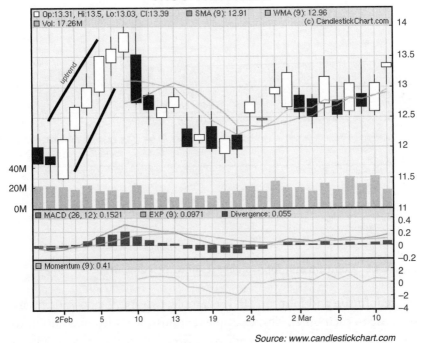

Source: www.candlestickchart.com

Figure 4.1 Yahoo chart showing an uptrend

In the case of Yahoo!, note the indicated area, which shows a six-day uptrend under the swing trading definition: new highs were higher than the previous day's high, and new lows were higher than the previous day's low. In this and other chart examples, the periods used are days; however, it is worth noting that some swing traders use much shorter periods, seeking these kinds of patterns in 15-minute and 5-minute charts, for example.

A *downtrend* is the opposite, with progressively lower prices, shown in Figure 4.2.

Johnson and Johnson chart

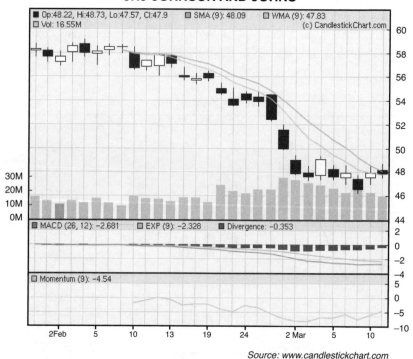

Source: www.candlestickchart.com

Figure 4.2   Johnson and Johnson chart showing a downtrend

In the Johnson and Johnson (JNJ) example, two specific downturns are set close to each other. This example demonstrates why, in addition to identifying the immediate trend, you also need to recognize a pattern swing traders call the *set-up*, which tells you when to enter or exit a position.

> **Key Point:** You can identify entry and exit points by tracking a pattern over three to five days.

The set-up is found at the top or bottom of the current trend. Look for any of three aspects to a trading pattern to identify the set-up. They may be found alone, but in combinations, the indication is quite strong. These set-ups are expected to develop within three to five days in a typical swing pattern. When you have all three signals at the same time, it is the strongest of all possible set-up signals. These signals are

1. *A reversal day.* The reversal day is the day when an established trend ends. The uptrend stops as soon as a downward-loving day occurs. This simply means that the stock's closing price is lower than its open, or vice versa. The Yahoo! uptrend in Figure 4.1 ended with a very strong reversal day. The Johnson and Johnson downtrend ended with a less sudden day moving upward.

2. *A narrow-range day, or NRD.* In this pattern, the day's trading range thins to a much smaller range than previously established. In a candlestick chart, this is shown as a smaller rectangle in the body of the trading day. For example, in Figure 4.2, the second downtrend ends when three consecutive days are followed by one day with a very narrow trading range. The NRD is an indicator that buyers and sellers have settled down to a general agreement that the established trend is ending. This is often followed by a reversal, as in the case of JNJ in Figure 4.2.

3. *High volume.* The second JNJ downtrend in Figure 4.2 is accompanied by growing daily volume. This peaked at the bottom of the downtrend and then began to fall off. In many patterns, the single high-volume day is far more pronounced than this.

When all three of these set-up signals are present at the same time, you have a very strong indicator, with the three signals confirming the set-up. The current trend and set-up signals are easily recognized with the use of candlestick charts.

> **Key Point:** Swing traders do not trade the company; they trade the stock. Short-term price volatility is the key to this strategy.

To briefly explain candlesticks: These charts consist of a series of daily activity showing all the information you need about a stock's price movement. The attributes of the candlestick formation are shown in Figure 4.3.

The candlestick

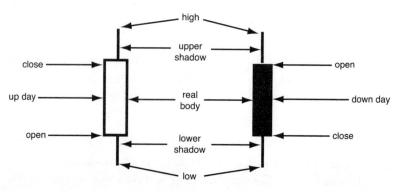

Figure 4.3   The candlestick and its attributes

The up-trending day is usually a white or clear chart, although some Web sites use variations of color. A downward-moving day is black or, when other colors are used, a darker color than the upward day. The "body" or rectangle summarizes the trading range for the day; the upper edge of the rectangle is the closing price (in an up day) or the opening (in a down day). The lower edge is the opposite: the opening in an up day and the closing in a down day. Extensions above and below are the shadows; these represent the full trading range for the day; in most cases, daily prices extend above and below the open and close, so the shadows provide important information about a stock's daily volatility.

Candlesticks are popular because they show, at a glance, the action for the day, not only regarding price volatility, but trading direction and opening and closing price levels. Compared to the open, high, low, close (OHLC) chart, the candlestick is a much more practical device for swing trading. And in today's Internet environment, candlestick charts are widely available on many free sites that provide charting information.

A Swing Trading Method: Long and Short Stock

The swing trader who uses a traditional approach will buy shares of stock at the bottom of the downtrend and then sell at the top. The swing trader will short stock at the top and buy to close at the bottom. Once a position is exited, the swing trader waits for a new set-up. If the trader is in a position, the exit set-up does not usually serve as an entry set-up going in the opposite direction. For that, you would wait for a buy set-up (consisting of three or more days setting up the trend, a narrow range day, and/or a reversal day).

> **Key Point:** When you swing trade with stock, you have to go long at the bottom and go short at the top of the price swing. If you don't want to short stock, you miss out on half of the swing trading opportunities.

Under the system using stock, you would enter a long position at the bottom of a downtrend or enter a short position at the end of an uptrend. The number of shares depends on your personal risk profile and also on the resources you have available. Using stock for swing trading always involves limits based on your capital resources, broker limits on margin (on the short sale side), and the level of risk you can afford. For this reason, many swing traders use odd lots for the strategy.

The selection of an appropriate stock is crucial in swing trading. Remember, swing traders are interested in the stock's volatility more than in the fundamental attributes of the company; it is a technical system. The ideal swing trading stock demonstrates a degree of moderate volatility. If the price volatility is too low, swing traders will not be able to get the short-term price movement needed to maximize the outcome. If volatility is too high, the set-up patterns are much less predictable.

Defining volatility relies on a study of the stock's trading range. You need to have enough swing in the highest to lowest prices of the range, as well as movement within the breadth of the range to offer an attractive price trend. In other words, even if the breadth of the trading range contains enough points to make the stock a good swing trading candidate, the daily price movement has to also be active enough to ensure that there will be movement.

Additionally, if you are aware of the strength in the technical attributes of a stock, you have a better grasp of which issues work as swing trading choices. Knowing about the strength or weakness of resistance and support, for example, helps you to confirm set-up signals. If a double top or head-and-shoulders pattern takes place, most technicians recognize these as foreshadowing a price movement downward. Likewise, a double bottom or reverse head-and-shoulders pattern often precedes a price uptrend. These basic patterns may be used to confirm the short-term set-ups you find using uptrend and downtrend tracking, narrow range days, high volume, and reversal days.

The Alternative: Using Options

Many traders abandon swing trading due to the market risks when using stock. The requirement to go short on half of the swing trading opportunities makes risk levels unacceptable. Many others limit swing trading only to downtrends as they bottom out. They buy shares of stock, wait for the sell set-up, and then get out of their positions. The problem with this approach is that it is not really swing trading; it is, instead, only a bull sentiment form of speculation.

> **Key Point:** A basic premise of swing trading is that you want to take advantage of uptrends *and* downtrends. This explains why options are lower-risk and higher-leverage vehicles for swings.

Realistically, you know that stock prices rise *and* fall, so it only makes sense to swing trade on both uptrends and downtrends. This gets around the tendency to view the market with an unrealistically optimistic point of view and sets up situations in which you can swing trade in *either* direction or in both directions. This doubles your profit opportunities.

Even so, the need to short stock for half of the swing trading opportunities is simply beyond the profile most people want to adopt. This is the place where options are valuable. Using options to swing trade instead of stocks cuts loss potential while enabling you to leverage capital—all without ever needing to go short. These are the essential attributes of a long option form of swing trading. Of course, more aggressive traders can also use short options and gain additional advantages. This approach is explained later.

Long Options

The simple long option strategy is based on the assumption that you limit your selection to very short-term contracts, those scheduled to expire within one month or less. In most options strategies, you require time for prices to develop, so the balance between time value and cost defines the long option strategy. In swing trading, the complete transaction is expected to take between three and five days, so using very short-term options makes sense, especially those right at the money or even slightly in the money.

> **Key Point:** Options traders normally prefer contracts with some time remaining until expiration. Swing trading is the exception. In this strategy, about-to-expire options work best.

For example, assume that two possible swing trading stocks—Yahoo! and Microsoft—had attractively low premiums at the money or close to ATM status, on a March trading session (nine trading days before expiration). If you expected movement within those nine sessions, using these options makes sense:

Yahoo! (YHOO) priced at $13.39

March 13 call	0.85
March 13 put	0.47

Microsoft (MSFT) priced at $17.11

March 17 call	0.60
March 17 put	0.49

In the case of Yahoo! there is no intrinsic value in the call, and the put contains only 39 cents of intrinsic value premium. Microsoft's call has 11 cents of intrinsic value, and there is no intrinsic value in the puts. These numbers are slight, however, and the chances for price movement are quite promising. In all these cases, it would take only slight movement in the stock by expiration day to produce a profit. For example, if you bought a Microsoft call and the stock rose to $18 per share by expiration day (89 points), intrinsic value would increase to $100, or 40 cents higher than the cost of 60 cents, a 66.7 percent return in nine trading days. This $40 profit is not a large amount of cash, but if the principle is applied using multiple options, profits can be quite large. A purchase of the Microsoft 17 put at 0.49 would grow to $100 in value if the stock fell to $16, a decrease of $1.11 per share. That would yield a profit of 51 cents per put.

Of course, these opportunities apply only if you spot a strong buy set-up within the period remaining until expiration. Because the use of long calls and puts creates buy set-up on both sides, you have twice the chance of spotting an opportunity. (The typical swing trading set-up is distinguished as a buy set-up or a sell set-up. But because you will use long puts in place of shorting stock, it is actually a put buy set-up. When you are using all long positions, there are no sell entry set-ups.)

> **Key Point:** When you swing trade with stock, you look for both buy and sell set-ups. But with long options, you deal only with buy set-ups, either for long calls or for long puts.

This strategy clearly offers less risk than using shares of stock. Because each option controls 100 shares, the equivalent with stock would require investments of about $1,300 in Yahoo! or $1,700 in Microsoft. The only advantage with this approach is that stock does not expire in nine days. However, because swing trading is intentionally short term, that consideration should not prevent you from recognizing the double advantage. Not only is the position highly leveraged (requiring investments under $100 in all possible situations); it is also low risk. You can never lose more than the premium. In the case of Yahoo! the maximum loss would be $85 for the long call or $47 for the long put. For Microsoft, the maximum loss would be $60 for the long call or $49 for the long put.

Why pick options scheduled to expire in nine trading sessions? With little or no intrinsic value, the short-term options are going to track movement in the stock more exactly than at any other time. Any increase in the stock price (for the call position) or decrease in the stock price (for the put position) is going to see a mirroring effect in the options, making these short-term positions perfect for swing trading.

All other options strategies involve long-term options, and the interactions between time value, intrinsic value, and extrinsic value are problematic for swing trading. The longer the time until expiration, the higher the time value *and* the less responsive the option will be to movement in the stock's price. Even when a long-term option is in the money, it will not always track price movement in the underlying on a point-for-point basis. This occurs because extrinsic value (the portion representing volatility and excluding intrinsic and time value) may adjust overall premium. This is notably true when the current value of the underlying moves closer to the option's strike. So longer-term options, with time value premium and tendency to under-react to price movement, are not appropriate for swing trading.

> **Key Point:** Swing trading is probably the only strategy for which close-to-expiring options are preferred over longer-term ones.

Variations on the Options Swing Trading Method

Even within the range of options, you can create several different strategies. To illustrate, begin by studying the range of options for one company, Target (TGT), based on a March timeline, as shown in Table 4.1.

Table 4.1   Target (TGT) $26.90: March Options

Strike	Calls	Puts
25	2.32	0.40
27.50	0.74	1.25
30	0.16	2.99

At the point Target was at $26.90 per share, a buy set-up occurred. After three days of a downtrend, a narrow range day was followed by an upward day (the narrow range day was so narrow, in fact, that the rectangle is reduced to only a thin horizontal line). This pattern is shown in Figure 4.4 (note the last four trading sessions).

Target chart

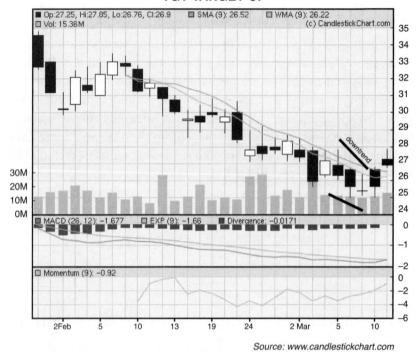

Source: www.candlestickchart.com

Figure 4.4   Target chart showing narrow range day as set-up signal

Using the long option version of options for swing trading, you would buy the March 27.50 call at this point; the cost is 0.74 ($74). Incidentally, if you had bought a put at the indicated top a few sessions earlier, this would also be the point of a sell set-up. Buying the March 27.50 call, which contains no intrinsic value, you need the stock's price to rise to $28.24 per share by expiration to break even and to exceed that price level to create a profit.

Short Options

A second way to employ options is to use only short positions in place of long positions. At the top of the swing cycle, you sell a call, and at the bottom, you close the call and sell a put. This alternative has the added feature of cash coming to you instead of being paid out. An extremely short-term life remaining to expiration is an advantage as well because the goal is to see short-term short options decline in value or expire worthless.

> **Key Point:** Depending on your risk tolerance, you can use either long options or short options to swing trade. This introduces interesting variations to the basic strategy.

Given the same facts as in the long option strategy, at the bottom of this cycle, you would close out a short call and replace it with a short put. If you had previously sold a 30 call, a buy to close requires only $16 based on the Target data; and a 27.50 put is then sold for 1.25 ($125). This approach is safest when you also own 100 shares of the underlying, based on several assumptions:

1. The short calls written at the top of the swing produce capital gains in the stock if exercised.

2. You are willing to acquire another 100 shares of the stock in the event the put is exercised.

3. The combined premium income from writing short calls justifies the risk in your opinion because it increases short-term income while playing the swings based on recognition of set-up signals.

Calls Only

Yet another method involves using only call options. You enter a long call at the bottom, closing it at the top of the swing, and you sell a call at the top, closing it at the bottom. Like the previous strategy, employing short calls is relatively safe if you own 100 shares of the underlying, because in the event of exercise, you simply deliver the shares of stock without having to make up the difference between strike and market price. For example, given the Target example, you may have previously sold a 30 call, which can now be closed at 0.16 ($16), and this is replaced with the purchase of a 27.50 call at 0.74 ($74). As the stock rises, intrinsic value of this call tracks the stock point for point.

> **Key Point:** Using calls on both sides of the swing enables you to go both long and short. This is low risk when you own 100 shares, meaning the short side is also a covered call.

Puts Only

You can also use puts exclusively. This is the opposite of using only calls. You enter a long put at the top of the price swing, knowing that intrinsic value will increase point for point with in-the-money declines in the stock. The long put is sold at the bottom of the price cycle. Entry at the bottom consists of a short put; the theory here relies on the belief in set-up signals that the stock's price will rise so that the short put can be closed at a profit. The use of short puts is appropriate only if you are willing to acquire 100 shares of the stock at the strike. In that event, your basis will consist of the strike minus the premium you receive for selling the put. For example, if you had bought a long 30 put a few sessions before the indicated date, it could be sold for 2.99 ($299). The long position is replaced at the bottom of the cycle with a short put. In this example, the 27.50 put can be sold for 1.25 ($125). As the stock price rises as part of the expected swing direction, the value of this about-to-expire put will decline rapidly and can be sold at a profit or just allowed to expire.

> **Key Point:** Just as you can use long and short calls, you can also swing trade with long and short puts. Because short puts are not as risky as short calls, this approach appeals to many swing traders.

Multiple Contract Strategies

You are not limited to the use of single options; in fact, swing trading can increase leverage when you sense an advantage in price momentum. If a stock's price, in your opinion, is going to make a strong move in either direction, you may consider one of many strategies using more than one option.

Multiple Contracts

In a multiple contract variation, you double up the number of options you open at either the top or bottom of a swing. This can be adjusted to reflect your belief about the overall price direction. For example, if you believe an upward trend is stronger than a downward trend, the swing strategy could involve buying one put at the swing top set-up, but buying two (or more) calls at the bottom. If you are correct in this opinion, the swing profit increases when you use multiples of the contract.

Even when you do not know whether the trend is focused upward or downward, you can certainly increase your swing positions by using multiple contracts on either side of the swing pattern. If you conclude that the set-ups are reliable, the multiple contract approach is practical, especially given the relatively cheap at-the-money options soon to expire. Without time value as a factor, these contracts are quite cheap; and as expiration gets close, the premium falls significantly. So when you have two weeks or less until expiration, an at-the-money option is probably the best bargain you can find for a leveraged strategy. As long as you are confident that the short-term trend is going to play out before expiration, this is a high-potential swing trading method.

> **Key Point:** If you sense a strong trend is coming, you can double up on your option positions. This increases your risk but also increases your profit potential.

Multiple Strikes

In addition to using multiple option contracts, you can develop a swing trade to take advantage of the ongoing trend. In most discussions of swing trading, the assumption is that you take up a position at a fixed moment in the price trend and wait for it to develop. But what if a trend is exceptionally strong?

In this scenario, you can increase your swing trading positions by buying calls (in an uptrend) or puts (in a downtrend) as the underlying stock's price reaches another strike plateau. This may be 2½, 5, or 10 points; the advantage is derived from buying into the trend. This assumes you approach swing trading using long options, but the same argument applies on the short side. If you are willing to take up the higher risks of short option positions, you would *sell* into the trend as it develops.

> **Key Point:** Traditional wisdom tells you to buy into a trend. The same argument applies to both sides of the swing trade. As prices move upward or downward, you can take up additional long call (uptrend) or put (downtrend) positions.

Spread or Straddle Conversion

In coming chapters, the particulars of spreads and straddles are analyzed in detail. For now, a swing trading strategy based on taking up a single position (in calls or puts, and either long or short) can also be changed into either a spread (options with different strikes, different expirations, or both) or a straddle (simultaneous opening of offsetting positions with the same strike). Considering the permutations of these strategies, you soon develop a universe of potentially profitable adjustments to a single swing trade position. Spreads and straddles may improve profit potential as short-term price trends max out; they may increase or decrease risk levels based on the status (long or short) of outstanding options; and they may convert a simple swing trade into a more complex collar or other advanced strategy.

> **Key Point:** Some swing trade posi-
> tions evolve into more advanced option
> strategies. This may either increase or
> decrease risk, depending on whether
> the expansion opens up long or short
> exposure.

Covered Ratio Write Swing

A covered ratio write swing is a strategy for increasing cash income as part of a swing trade. Using short options only, you sell calls at the top and sell puts at the bottom. If you own 100 shares for each call sold in this strategy, you have created a covered call. However, you can also increase income with a ratio write. In this strategy, you write more calls than you have covered. For example, if you own 200 shares and you sell three calls, you create a 3-to-1 ratio write.

At the bottom of the swing, you close out the short calls and replace them with short puts. The number depends on how much exposure you want to take. One way to define the appropriate number of short puts is to assume they will be exercised. In that case, how many increments of 100 shares are you willing to acquire at the put's strike?

You mitigate the risk of short puts (and short calls) by using rolling techniques. Although this does help avoid or delay exercise, it also extends risk exposure for a longer period. Given the basic advantage in swing trading with very short-term at-the-money options, the need to roll away from exercise contradicts the strategy and is not going to be appropriate for everyone. Keeping short positions open also continues the need for maintaining margin at minimum levels, restricting additional short option activity on other issues.

> **Key Point:** Creating a ratio on the
> short side as part of your swing trade
> opens up many possibilities, including
> greater profits and risks, and the
> potential need to roll forward to defer
> or avoid exercise.

Long and Short Combination

A final strategy combines long and short option positions at both sides of the short-term price swing. This strategy has the advantage of reducing the cost of taking long positions because the credit from the short offsets the debit from the long side. If part of the strategy also includes a covered call, the risk level is greatly reduced.

The strategy involves buying calls and selling puts at the bottom of the swing, and buying puts and selling calls at the top. This has the same general result as doubling up a long position, but the cost offset makes the strategy more affordable. For example, returning to the example of Target when the stock price was $26.90, an opening swing trade at the bottom of the cycle would combine the long 27.50 call and the short 27.50 put:

27.50 call	0.74
27.50 put	− 1.25
Net Credit	− 0.51

In this example, you create a small credit; trading cost will reduce this to close to break-even. However, you have doubled up at the buy set-up with a no-cost spread. As the stock rises, the put loses value and the call gains. If the stock's price falls, the long call becomes worthless and the short put is exercised (or rolled forward to avoid exercise). But because the net cost is zero, if profit does not develop by expiration, nothing is actually lost.

> **Key Point:** You create a no-cost, low-cost, or small credit position when you swing trade with combinations of long and short at the same time. This strategy can be structured with little or no market risk.

If a similar approach is employed at the top of the swing, the opposite tactic applies. For example, if you faced a sell set-up (this is the normal description of the moment when you would sell stock in anticipation of a downtrend), you would buy the put and sell the call. Given the same price level, this results in a net cost of 0.51 ($51) plus trading costs. This is quite small and is close to a no-cost strategy. If the stock's price does decline, the short call's value diminishes as the long put picks up value.

The combo is virtually a no-risk approach if you also own 100 shares. In this case, the spread consists of a short call and a long put. The short call, if exercised, is covered by 100 shares of stock, and the long put may expire worthless if the stock price rises or will gain value if it falls. But given the fact that this is close to a no-cost position, the covered call side is safe and, for nearly no cost, this doubles up your swing trading position.

Including all strategies, there are at least nine ways to swing trade with options. They are

1. Long options

2. Short options

3. Calls only

4. Puts only

5. Multiple contracts

6. Multiple strikes

7. Spread or straddle conversion

8. Covered ratio write swing

9. Long and short combination

In the next chapter, the possibilities for puts are expanded into the world of long spreads. In this type of spread, long options are used; this reduces market risk because you can never lose more than the actual premium you pay. At the same time, the cost of the options does reduce potential gains. The combination of premium costs and the need to overcome time value premium before expiration makes the long spread a challenging strategy, but using methods to time long spreads effectively gives you a clear advantage.

5

PUT STRATEGIES FOR SPREADS: HEDGING FOR PROFIT

U sing single options, either long or short, to create basic strategies involves many possible variations. Whether used to hedge other positions or simply to speculate, options trading based on one-contract strategies is widely popular. But when you go beyond this and begin thinking about the many ways to set up *spreads*, the options universe gets much larger and offers greater potential for leverage and profits.

Spreads—opening two or more option positions with different strikes, different expiration dates, or both—come in many varieties and present opportunities to use puts profitably. With emphasis on call-based spreads, puts are easily overlooked. However, it makes more sense to view calls and puts as equals, advantageous in different situations. Both can be used to create profits, hedge risk, and generate cash.

This chapter analyzes the effective use of puts in many situations: bear, bull, calendar, diagonal, and combination strategies. The purpose is to demonstrate that in any kind of market, a spread strategy can be designed to match your risk profile suitably and to take advantage of time value trends without increasing market risk exposure.

Bear Spreads

The *bear spread* is created with a short put at a strike price below a long put. This creates a net debit because the higher-strike put will always have a higher premium at the same expiration price. A corresponding bear spread using calls sets up a credit spread and consists of a lower short call and a higher long call (the lower, short call will always have a higher premium, thus creating a bear spread using calls).

A bear spread employing either puts or calls has the same profit potential, and the only differences are credit versus debit and variation in levels of risk. With calls, the more valuable short contract is at risk of exercise; and if exercised, it is difficult to make up the difference between short and long strike without taking some loss. With puts, the lower short put is less at risk and is more effectively covered by the higher long position.

> **Key Point:** Spreads are described as
> "bear" when the short put's strike is
> lower than the long put's strike.

An example of a bear spread using puts: U.S. Steel traded for $17.91 per share and at that time four-month puts were available in increments above and below that price:

Buy 20 put	$5.70
Sell 17.50 put	4.40
Net debit	$1.30

For a net debit of $130, the bear put spread is opened. If the stock's price were to rise, the 17.50 put would lose value; if the stock remains above 17.50, it will expire worthless. However, the more expensive long put at 20 will increase in value only if the stock's price declines. The best outcome would be for the stock's price to decline below both strikes. In that instance, the 1.30 point cost would be offset by the advantageous 2.50 point spread, as shown in Table 5.1.

Table 5.1   U.S. Steel ($17.91)

Price per Share	Long 20 Put	Short 17.50 Put	Net
		Profit or Loss at Expiration	
$20	$–570	$ 440	$–130
19	–470	440	– 30
18	–370	440	70

Table 5.1 Continued

Price per Share	Profit or Loss at Expiration		
	Long 20 Put	Short 17.50 Put	Net
17	−270	390	120
16	−170	290	120
15	− 70	190	120
14	30	90	120
13	130	− 10	120
12	230	−110	120

The bear put spread in this example fixes the maximum loss at the initial debit of $130, and fixes the maximum profit at $120. This occurs if and when the underlying stock's price falls below $18 per share. The bear put spread using these values is summarized in Figure 5.1.

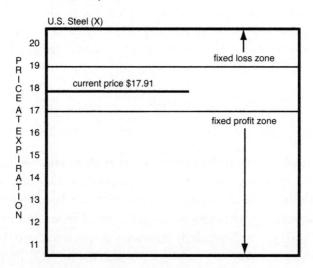

Figure 5.1 Bear Put Spread, U.S. Steel

In bear spreads with puts, the maximum loss is never greater than the net debit (before calculating trading costs). The maximum profit is always the net of the difference between strikes minus the initial debit (in the example, 2.50 points minus 1.30 points, or 1.20, $120). And the point of breakeven is equal to the higher strike price minus the debit (in this case, 20 minus 1.30, or breakeven at 18.70 per share).

> **Key Point:** The maximum loss in a put-based bear spread is never higher than the net debit you pay for opening the position.

The primary advantage to entering a put bear spread over the call bear spread is that the short put is going to be out of the money. So there is no risk of early exercise as long as the short put remains above strike. With the call bear spread, you earn a credit when you open the position, but the short call is in the money. This increases your risk of early exercise, which may occur before the position has a chance of producing a profit.

If the underlying stock's price drops rapidly and far enough, both long and short puts will be in the money. The loss of extrinsic value in the long put may exceed the same loss in the short put, maximizing the potential profit. The prices shown in the example for U.S. Steel are based on values upon expiration, but in the four months between now and then, variation in total premium is likely to favor the put bear spread net value to a greater degree than it would in the call-based bear spread.

Bull Spreads

A *bull spread* always involves selling a higher strike and buying a lower strike. This applies to both call-based and put-based bill spreads. With the put, the bull spread creates a net credit because the higher strike will always be worth more than a lower-strike put. The maximum profit is accomplished when the underlying stock's price rises above the higher strike, taking it out of the money. Although the profit is limited, it is assured. The maximum possible loss is limited to the difference between the two strike prices minus the credit received when the spread is opened.

An example of a put-based bull spread: Google (GOOG) had a market price of $318.97 per share. At that time, three-month puts could be used to create a bull spread:

Sell 320 put	33.30
Buy 310 put	28.10
Net credit	5.20

In this case, maximum profit is never greater than the credit received, or $520. And the maximum loss is calculated as follows:

Higher strike	320
Less: lower strike	−310
Strike difference	10
Less: credit received	− 5.20
Maximum loss	4.80

Table 5.2 shows the outcome at various expiration-day stock prices for this bull spread.

Table 5.2 Google ($318.97)

| | | Profit or Loss at Expiration | |
Price per Share	Long 320 Put	Short 310 Put	Net
$327	$3,330	$−2,810	$ 520
326	3,330	−2,810	520
325	3,330	−2,810	520
324	3,330	−2,810	520
323	3,330	−2,810	520
322	3,330	−2,810	520
321	3,330	−2,810	520
320	3,330	−2,810	520
319	3,230	−2,810	420
318	3,130	−2,810	320
317	3,030	−2,810	220
316	2,930	−2,810	120

Table 5.2   Continued

Price per Share	Long 320 Put	Short 310 Put	Net
		Profit or Loss at Expiration	
315	2,830	−2,810	20
314	2,730	−2,810	− 80
313	2,630	−2,810	− 180
312	2,530	−2,810	− 280
311	2,430	−2,810	− 380
310	2,330	−2,810	− 480
309	2,230	−2,710	− 480
308	2,130	−2,610	− 480
307	2,030	−2,510	− 480

Figure 5.2 shows how the fixed profit and loss zones work out in this example of the put bull spread.

Bull Put Spread

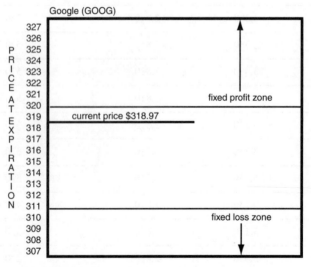

Figure 5.2   Bull Put Spread, Google

PUT OPTION STRATEGIES FOR SMARTER TRADING

Key Point: The maximum profit in a
put-based bull spread is never higher
than the net credit you receive when
the position is opened.

Just as potential profit and risk were both limited in the put-based bear spread, both are equally limited in the bull spread. In the example of Google, there are 10 point increments between strike prices due to the high market value of the stock. Option premium levels are also considerably higher than in stocks worth less than $100. The relationships are neither better nor worse when stock prices are higher. The scale of value between options is not affected by price level as much as by the stock's trading range volatility.

Calendar Spreads

A *calendar spread* (also called a *time spread*) has different expiration dates and identical strikes. It is often described as "horizontal." This is a distinction from the more common vertical spreads (with identical expirations but different strike prices).

In its usual configuration, the option closest to expiration is sold, and the one further away is bought in the calendar spread. This is true whether puts or calls are used to create the position.

Key Point: In a calendar spread, the
closest expiration option is always
short and the option further away is
long, whether puts or calls are used.

A put calendar spread can be opened with the intention of closing the short position at or near expiration and taking the profit, and leaving the longer-term long put open in the hopes of future profits. The maximum profit occurs when the underlying stock is near the strike but out of the money at the short expiration and then falls in value so that the long position becomes profitable. This strategy makes sense because shorter-term option time value always falls more rapidly than time value for longer-term options. However, because the calendar spread involves a debit, the combination of profits on both short and long puts is not always easy to achieve. The most likely outcome is to close the short positions with enough profit to cover the debit and then wait to see how the long puts perform or to simply close out the long positions as well.

The maximum gain is positive; for example, if the short position is closed and the long position subsequently gains due to a rapid decline in the underlying stock's value, both options could be profitable. At the same time, the maximum loss in the calendar spread is always limited to the initial debit (plus trading costs). The only exception to this limited loss occurs if and when you sell the long position before the short. This would occur if the stock's price fell enough for the long put to become profitable, but the problem in selling and leaving the in-the-money short put open is that it loses the cover gained in the spread and makes exercise likely. In that event, the loss on the short is equal to the difference between the short put's strike and the exercise price minus the short premium received.

Example of a calendar spread: United Parcel Service (UPS) had a market value of $43.01 when the one-month 45 put was worth 3.40 and the four-month 45 put was worth 4.80. A calendar spread consists of

Sell one-month 45 put	$ 340
Buy four-month 45 put	−480
Net debit	$−140

One way to think of the calendar spread is that it provides a very cheap long put. If you were to simply buy the four-month put, it would cost $480. The calendar spread limits maximum loss to the $140 debit, and if the short expires, you net out with a four-month put for a far cheaper premium.

The profit and loss zones for these two puts are shown in Table 5.3. However, be aware that because expiration dates are different, this position (more than most) actually consists of a short put covered by a later-expiring long put, so it really is more like two different positions than one that co-exist on the same underlying stock.

Table 5.3   United Parcel Service ($43.01)

Price per Share	Short 1-mo 45 Put	Long 3-mo 45 Put	Net
	Profit or Loss at Expiration		
$50	$340	$-480	$-140
49	340	-480	-140
48	340	-480	-140
47	340	-480	-140
46	340	-480	-140
45	340	-480	-140
44	240	-380	-140
43	140	-280	-140
42	40	-180	-140
41	-60	- 80	-140
40	-160	20	-140
39	-260	120	-140
38	-360	220	-140
37	-460	320	-140

Note that the indicated net loss is $140 at any price. This would be applicable if both puts expired on the same date. However, because the key to this strategy is the different expirations, the net overall maximum loss is just that, the maximum. The short is covered by the long. Profit can and does occur when the short expires or is closed at a profit, or when the short expires and then the long put increases in value.

The latter portion of this is not really necessary for the calendar spread
to become profitable. For example, if the underlying stock's value rose
to exactly $45 per share just before expiration, the short position would
be likely to fall in value to a very small level of time value. If the short
fell to 0.50, it could be closed at a profit:

Initial short sale	$340
Less: buy to close price	− 50
Profit on short put	$290

Since the initial position involved a debit of $140, closing the short cre-
ates a net overall profit of $150 ($290 − $140). Upon closing the short
put, you are left with the long put, which can be closed for its time value
or left to ride until expiration. This is the most desirable outcome of all
for the calendar spread: an overall profit from selling the short side,
resulting in a "free" long position that can either be closed or continued
for two more months. Because the long put's time value is likely to
decline rapidly at this point, selling it maximizes the profit, assuming
the stock's price will not decline adequately to offset current time value.

The strategy combines a fixed maximum profit and growing loss
potential for the short put, with a fixed maximum loss and growing
profit potential for the long put. This is illustrated in Figure 5.3.

This figure shows how the calendar spread creates profit potential. The
short's growing loss zone is offset by the opposite profit zone of the
long position, but it expires sooner. The combination of deterioration
in time value and the longer period of the long put is the place where
the advantage is gained in this position.

Calendar Spread

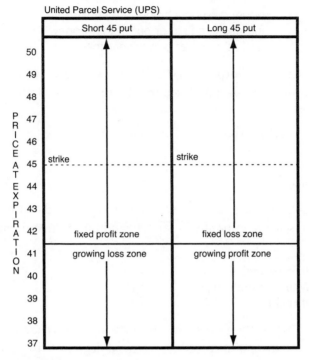

Figure 5.3   Calendar Spread, UPS

Diagonal Spread Strategies

The horizontal calendar spread and the better-known vertical spread patterns can be combined to create *diagonal spreads*. The horizontal involves the same strike but different expirations, and the vertical consists of different strikes and the same expiration. In the diagonal spread, both expiration and strike are different.

As in the calendar spread, the short put expires sooner than the long put. The position may be either a debit or a credit, based on whether the later-expiring long put has a higher expiration or a lower one. It also is determined by whether the long put is in the money (lower than the short) or out of the money (higher than the short).

Example: Chevron Corporation (CVX) was valued at $63.04 per share
when the one-month and three-month puts showed the following
premiums:

One-month 60 put	2.07
One-month 65 put	4.40
Three-month 60 put	4.19
Three-month 65 put	6.40

Two possible put diagonal spreads can be created based on this range of
puts. First, sell a one-month 65 for 4.40 and buy a three-month 60 for
4.19:

Sell one-month 65 put	4.40
Buy three-month 60 put	– 4.19
Net credit	0.21

Given the transaction fees, this is virtually a breakeven position.
However, the five-point spread represents a degree of risk. If the short
put is exercised at 65, coverage from the long 60 put is short by $500;
however, the premium from selling this put is 4.40 points, so the real
short put risk is far lower.

This strategy produces maximum profit if time value evaporates rapidly in the one-month put, which will occur as long as the stock's price
moves up. At the time of this transaction, the stock was about two
points in the money (63.04 versus strike of 65 for the short). The protection level for this situation is at $60.60 per share. This means that as
long as the stock remains at or above $60.60, the short put is not at risk
(65 strike minus short premium of 4.40 = breakeven price, 60.60).
When this is considered next to the longer term of the long put, the net
risk is not great.

If the put can be closed—even in the middle—at a profit, you are able
to acquire the three-month long put for no net cost. For example, if the
stock price remains at $63 until the day of expiration, the intrinsic

value of the short put would be 2 ($200). If closed at this point (assuming it has not been exercised), the profit on the short trade would be $240 (4.40 − 2.00). After this, the long put remains available to hold or to sell. But when you realize the $240 profit on the short put, the overall profit on the transaction is $263 ($240 + $21) minus trading costs.

A summary of the overall transaction in this diagonal spread is shown in Table 5.4.

Table 5.4   Chevron Corporation ($63.04)

| Price per Share | Profit or Loss at Expiration | | |
	Short 1-mo 65 Put	Long 3-mo 60 Put	Net
$70	$440	$−419	$ 21
69	440	−419	21
68	440	−419	21
67	440	−419	21
66	440	−419	21
65	440	−419	21
64	340	−419	− 79
63	240	−419	−179
62	140	−419	−279
61	40	−419	−379
60	− 60	−419	−479
59	−160	−319	−479
58	−260	−219	−479
57	−360	−119	−479
56	−460	− 19	−479
55	−560	81	−479
54	−660	181	−479

Table 5.4 Continued

Price per Share	Short 1-mo 65 Put	Long 3-mo 60 Put	Net
		Profit or Loss at Expiration	
53	−760	281	−479
52	−860	381	−479
51	−960	481	−479

The maximum gain of $21 and maximum loss of $479 are not applicable if, in fact, you manage this diagonal spread properly. Remember, the short time value will evaporate more rapidly than the long because it expires sooner. So the premium level will fall more quickly than the long put's, meaning the profit potential is significant. Table 5.4 represents net valuation as of the expiration date. Maximum loss is the five-point difference in strikes minus the initial credit of $21. This outcome is summarized in Figure 5.4.

> **Key Point:** Diagonal spreads are well suited for the strategy of profiting from the short side due to falling time value, leaving the long side open or closing it at a smaller profit.

This variation of the calendar spread creates a varying middle zone, due to the different expiration dates. In comparison, when the calendar spread is turned around with a long strike above the short rather than below it, the outcome is different. For example, if you sold the one-month 60 put and bought the three-month 65 put, the net debit would be

Sell one-month 60 put	−2.07
Buy three-month 65 put	6.40
Net debit	−4.33

Diagonal Spread

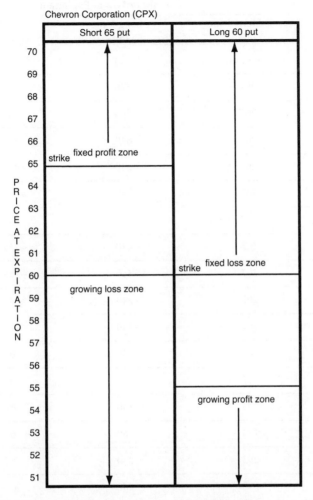

Figure 5.4   Diagonal Spread, Chevron Corp. – net credit

Now the diagonal put creates a debit; however, because the short side is three points out of the money, the exercise risk is low. In fact, exercise is protected down to a stock price of 57.93 per share (strike of 60 minus credit of 2.07 = 57.93). This is the breakeven of the short position by itself. However, because the long position is in the money by two points, intrinsic value will rise point for point with a declining value in the underlying. The outcome of this diagonal spread is shown in Table 5.5.

Table 5.5   Chevron Corporation (CVX), $63.04 Per Share

Price per Share	Short 1-mo 60 Put	Profit or Loss at Expiration Long 3-mo 65 Put	Net
$70	$207	$–640	$–433
69	207	–640	–433
68	207	–640	–433
67	207	–640	–433
66	207	–640	–433
65	207	–640	–433
64	207	–540	–333
63	207	–440	–233
62	207	–340	–133
61	207	–240	– 33
60	207	–140	67
59	107	– 40	67
58	7	60	67
57	– 93	160	67
56	–193	260	67
55	–293	360	67
54	–393	460	67
53	–493	560	67
52	–593	660	67
51	–693	760	67

In this version of the diagonal spread, the profit zone is found at the lower prices, and the maximum loss zone is in the upper price range. Both are fixed in combination, although they consist of fixed zones at the top, with an increasing loss zone (for the short put) and an increasing profit zone (for the long put) at the lower price ranges. Just as in the previous example, the short put expires sooner, so time value will decline more rapidly as well. The net debit was $433, so if the short put declines even to zero, maximum profit would be only $207; overall, the loss in the event of expiration of the short put remains at $226 ($433 − $207). However, if the total strategy is viewed in its separate parts, the longer-term long put and its growing profit zone in the event of a price decline present a good opportunity for profit.

The profitability in the event of a price increase or decrease in the underlying is usually characterized as a bull or bear diagonal spread. Under that definition, the first example is a bull spread because, overall, the profit zone is found at the top; and the second example is a bear diagonal spread because the profit zone is at the bottom. However, this definition is inaccurate due to the disparate expiration dates. In both examples, as long as the underlying remains at or above the strike of the short put, it can be closed at a profit; and then, ideally, if the underlying stock's price declines, the long put can also become profitable. Both strategies rely on a short-term bull posture and a longer-term bear posture for the stock. The outcome of the strategy is illustrated in Figure 5.5.

> **Key Point:** A diagonal spread cannot be called "bull" or "bear" accurately because earlier expiration changes the structure of the position entirely. Like many spreads, it is neither bull nor bear, but based on hedging risk while exploiting declining short option time value.

Diagonal Spread

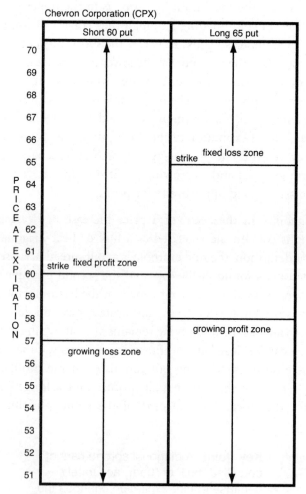

Figure 5.5   Diagonal Spread, Chevron Corp. – net debit

Combination Put Spreads

In addition to creating spreads with puts, you can also combine puts and calls for more complex variations, with different degrees of risk and ranges of potential profit or loss. The butterfly spread is called a neutral position because it offers limited risks in exchange for limited profits. It involves the simultaneous opening of a bull spread and a bear spread.

The butterfly spreads can be constructed in four different configurations:

>Call bull spread and call bear spread
>Call bull spread and put bear spread
>Put bull spread and call bear spread
>Put bull spread and put bear spread

Three strike prices are also involved. One of the two spreads includes the highest and middle strikes, and the other includes options at the middle and lowest strikes. For example, when IBM's stock was at $89.79 (closest to the 90 option strike), the following four-month options were available:

strike	calls	puts
85	10.80	6.39
90	8.00	9.00
95	5.80	11.50

A butterfly spread could be created in any of the four configurations based on these four variations:

Call Bull Spread and Call Bear Spread (Call-Call)

In the call bull spread and call bear spread scenario, two middle calls are sold and upper and lower calls are bought:

Buy one 85 call	−10.80
Sell two 90 calls	16.00
Buy one 95 call	− 5.80
Net debit	− 0.60

The outcome at these values is shown in Table 5.6.

Table 5.6   IBM Corporation ($89.79)—(Call-Call Spread)

Price per Share	Long 1 85 Call	Short 2 90 Calls	Long 1 95 Call	Net
		Profit or Loss at Expiration		
$ 102	$ 620	$– 8.00	$ 120	$ – 60
101	520	$– 6.00	20	– 60
100	420	$– 4.00	– .80	– 60
99	320	– 2.00	– 180	– 60
98	220	0	– 280	– 60
97	120	2.00	– 380	– 60
96	20	4.00	– 480	– 60
95	– 80	6.00	– 580	– 60
94	– 180	8.00	– 580	40
93	– 280	10.00	– 580	140
92	– 380	12.00	– 580	240
91	– 480	14.00	– 580	340
90	– 580	16.00	– 580	440
89	– 680	16.00	– 580	340
88	– 780	16.00	– 580	240
87	– 880	16.00	– 580	140
86	– 980	16.00	– 580	40
85	–1,080	16.00	– 580	– 60
84	–1,080	16.00	– 580	– 60
83	–1,080	16.00	– 580	– 60
82	–1,080	16.00	– 580	– 60
81	–1,080	16.00	– 580	– 60
80	–1,080	16.00	– 580	– 60

This butterfly spread sets up a limited loss equal to the original debit, existing above and below a middle range. The middle range is profitable, with maximum profit at the price of $90, or the middle-range strike. This is also illustrated in Figure 5.6.

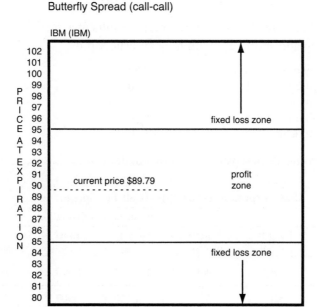

Figure 5.6   Butterfly Spread (call-call), IBM

The call-call spread can also be flipped to create a small credit and reverse the profit and loss zones. The reverse position involves

Sell one 85 call	10.80
Buy two 90 calls	−16.00
Sell one 95 call	5.80
Net credit	0.60

> **Key Point:** Any spread can be flipped, turning debit into credit and vice versa; this also flips the likely outcome at each profit or loss zone.

This variation creates limited profit zones above and below the middle that can never exceed the net credit, and a loss zone in the middle range. Considering that transaction costs offset most of the credit in this example, the strategy is of questionable value. However, it is one of the many possibilities in the combined spread universe.

Call Bull Spread and Put Bear Spread (Call-Put)

The call bull spread and put bear spread results in a net debit and combines long and short calls with long and short puts:

Buy one 85 call	−10.80
Sell one 90 call	8.00
Buy one 95 put	−11.50
Sell one 90 put	9.00
Net debit	− 5.30

The outcome at these values is shown in Table 5.7.

Table 5.7   IBM Corporation ($89.79)—(Call-Put Spread)

Price per Share	Long 1 85 Call	Short 1 90 Calls	Long 1 95 Put	Short 1 90 Put	Net
			Profit or Loss at Expiration		
$ 102	$ 620	$–400	$–1,150	$ 900	$ – 30
101	520	– 300	–1,150	900	– 30
100	420	– 200	–1,150	900	– 30
99	320	– 100	–1,150	900	– 30
98	220	0	–1,150	900	– 30
97	120	100	–1,150	900	– 30
96	20	200	–1,150	900	– 30
95	– 80	300	–1,150	900	– 30
94	– 180	400	–1,050	900	70
93	– 280	500	– 950	900	170
92	– 380	600	– 850	900	270
91	– 480	700	– 750	900	370
90	– 580	800	– 650	900	470

Table 5.7   Continued

Price per Share	Long 1 85 Call	Short 1 90 Calls	Long 1 95 Put	Short 1 90 Put	Net
			Profit or Loss at Expiration		
89	− 680	800	− 550	800	370
88	− 780	800	− 450	700	270
87	− 880	800	− 350	600	170
86	− 980	800	− 250	500	70
85	−1,080	800	− 150	400	− 30
84	−1,080	800	− 50	300	− 30
83	−1,080	800	50	200	− 30
82	−1,080	800	150	100	− 30
81	−1,080	800	250	0	− 30
80	−1,080	800	350	− 100	− 30

This strategy is not a wise one on its surface. It costs $530 to enter, but the maximum possible profit is only $470. And although maximum losses are limited to only $30, holding all positions until closing would never produce a net yield. The reason the maximum loss is five points below the original debit is the differences in strike prices. The five-point spread offsets long and short, reducing the likely maximum loss from $530 down to only $30. On the profit side, the maximum of $470 versus original debit of $530 reflects the maximum distance of 10 points between highest and lowest position.

> **Key Point:** Butterfly spreads limit risk but also limit profit. Before you open this complex position, it makes sense to also work up an exit strategy to maximize profits by selling shorts to cover the initial debit.

The strategy could be profitable if the short positions could be closed before expiration at a profit, and if the long positions subsequently also became profitable. This would require the underlying stock to act in the required manner or for time value in short positions to decline rapidly, and then for one or the other long positions to benefit from a sharp movement in the stock. It is possible, if only due to a decline in short time value coupled with remaining premium value in the long options.

This position is illustrated in Figure 5.7.

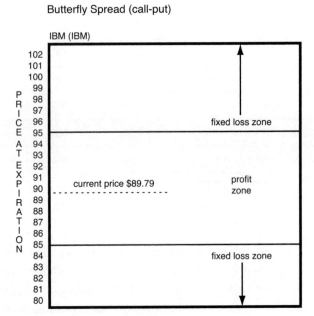

Figure 5.7   Butterfly Spread (call-put), IBM

The profit and loss zones for this strategy are identical to those for the call-based butterfly; however, the profit potential is not as good.

The position can also be reversed:

Sell one 85 call	10.80
Buy one 90 call	– 8.00
Sell one 95 put	11.50
Buy one 90 put	– 9.00
Net credit	5.30

This spread creates a limited profit zone above and below, with a loss zone in the middle. Even though the $530 credit is preferable over the debit, this version of the butterfly can become profitable only if the short sides can be closed advantageously once time value has declined.

Put Bull Spread and Call Bear Spread (Put-Call)

A net credit results when you combine put bull and call bear spreads into a butterfly formation. For example:

Buy one 85 put	– 6.39
Sell one 90 put	9.00
Buy one 95 call	– 5.80
Sell one 90 call	9.00
Net credit	5.81

Table 5.8 summarizes the outcome for this butterfly spread.

Table 5.8   IBM Corporation ($89.79)—(Put-Call Spread)

Price per Share	Long 1 85 Put	Short 1 90 Put	Long 1 95 Call	Short 1 90 Call	Net
			Profit or Loss at Expiration		
$102	$– 639	$ 900	$ 120	$–300	$ 81
101	– 639	900	20	–200	81
100	– 639	900	– 80	–100	81
99	– 639	900	–180	0	81
98	– 639	900	–280	100	81
97	– 639	900	–380	200	81
96	– 639	900	–480	300	81
95	– 639	900	–580	400	81
94	– 639	900	–580	500	181
93	– 639	900	–580	600	281
92	– 639	900	–580	700	381
91	– 639	900	–580	800	481
90	– 639	900	–580	900	581
89	– 639	800	–580	900	481
88	– 639	700	–580	900	381
87	– 639	600	–580	900	281

Table 5.8 Continued

Price per Share	Long 1 85 Put	Short 1 90 Put	Long 1 95 Call	Short 1 90 Call	Net
	Profit or Loss at Expiration				
86	− 639	500	−580	900	181
85	− 639	400	−580	900	81
84	− 539	300	−580	900	81
83	− 439	200	−580	900	81
82	− 339	100	−580	900	81
81	− 239	0	−580	900	81
80	− 139	− 100	−580	900	81

This butterfly not only creates a net credit, but also produces a limited profit up to the maximum of the credit itself. The position is summarized in Figure 5.8.

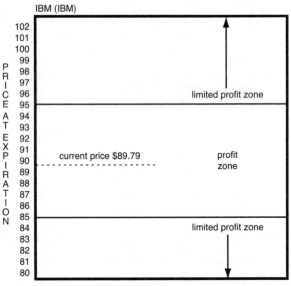

Figure 5.8   Butterfly Spread (put-call), IBM

Key Point: Some spreads create net profit at all price levels, although the extent is limited. Even so, such a position is still maximized when time value falls and short positions are closed or expire.

If you reverse the position, you would create an undesirable outcome:

Sell one 85 put	6.39
Buy one 90 put	− 9.00
Sell one 95 call	5.80
Buy one 90 call	− 9.00
Net debit	− 5.81

The outcome creates a loss at any price; it is limited above and below the middle but cannot produce a profit at any price. However, the position makes sense if the strategy is to wait out the time value in the two short positions (while reducing short risk with the two long options), intending to close these at a profit or close one short and let the other expire. The two long positions remain, and one may become profitable if the stock is enough points above the call strike or below the put strike. It is also possible to create a profit from a combination of reduced short time value and remaining long option value, but opening a butterfly that produces a loss at any price makes sense only if you rely on significant decline in the time value premium. In the example, both short options are worth 9.00 points, but it will still take a lot of movement to offset the time value of both long options.

Put Bull Spread and Put Bear Spread (Put-Put)

The final version of the combined straddle is based solely on the use of puts. The put bull spread and put bear spread involves the following positions:

Buy one 85 put	− 6.39
Sell two 90 puts	18.00
Buy one 95 put	−11.50
Net credit	0.11

The small net credit will be more than offset by trading costs, so this is close to a zero-credit position. The outcome is shown in Table 5.9.

Table 5.9 IBM Corporation ($89.79)—(Put-Put Spread)

Price per Share	Long 1 85 Put	Short 2 90 Puts	Long 1 95 Put	Net
		Profit or Loss at Expiration		
$102	$– 639	$1,800	$–1,150	$ 11
101	– 639	1,800	–1,150	11
100	– 639	1,800	–1,150	11
99	– 639	1,800	–1,150	11
98	– 639	1,800	–1,150	11
97	– 639	1,800	–1,150	11
96	– 639	1,800	–1,150	11
95	– 639	1,800	–1,150	11
94	– 639	1,800	–1,050	111
93	– 639	1,800	– 950	211
92	– 639	1,800	– 850	311
91	– 639	1,800	– 750	411
90	– 639	1,800	– 650	511
89	– 639	1,600	– 550	411
88	– 639	1,400	– 450	311
87	– 639	1,200	– 350	211
86	– 639	1,000	– 250	111
85	– 639	800	– 150	11
84	– 539	600	– 50	11
83	– 439	400	50	11
82	– 339	200	150	11
81	– 239	0	250	11

This strategy is illustrated in Figure 5.9.

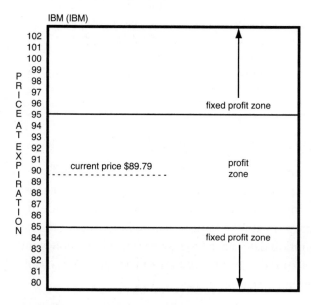

Figure 5.9   Butterfly Spread (put-put), IBM

The position can also be reversed, creating a net debit:

Sell one 85 put	6.39
Buy two 90 puts	−18.00
Sell one 95 put	11.50
Net debit	− 0.11

This version also creates losses at every price. However, as in the previous case, the position makes sense if you expect a decline in the short time value adequate to offset the net cost (which in this case is minimal). In fact, it is quite likely that the position could be converted to a profitable outcome by waiting out the decline in time value of the middle puts. At 18 points, that time value is considerable. If the stock were to finish up above the 90 strike, profit from the short puts would be considerable. A 10-point in-the-money status at expiration still leaves $800 profit, assuming no remaining time value. The position has high potential when the offsetting positions are viewed with the time value in mind. The long positions provide cover against the risk of exercise in the short puts, but the overall position will be profitable as long as the stock price does not fall more than 18 points below the 90 strike.

The Diagonal Butterfly Spread

By definition, a diagonal position must contain different strikes and
different expirations. The diagonal butterfly strategy has an earlier date
consisting of a straddle (see the next chapter); this means a short call
and a short put with the same strike are both sold. At the same time, the
later-expiration date is used to buy an out-of-the money put (at a strike
below the straddle strike) *and* an out-of-the money call (at a strike
above the short straddle strike).

For example, Best Buy (BBY) was valued at $29.65 and the following
options were available with expirations ½ and 3 ½ months away:

strike	calls	puts
½ month:		
30	0.85	1.15
3½ months:		
25		0.95
35	0.65	

The diagonal butterfly spread is constructed by shorting the call and
put closest to expiration (creating a short straddle) and buying the put
and call expiring further away. The net credit for this position is

Sell ½ month 30 call	0.85
Sell ½ month 30 put	1.15
Buy 3 ½ month 25 put	– 0.95
Buy 3 ½ month 35 call	– 0.65
Net credit	0.40

The outcome of this spread at different prices for the underlying is summarized in Table 5.10.

Table 5.10 Best Buy ($29.69) Diagonal Butterfly Spread

	Profit or Loss at Expiration				
	½ Month		3½ Month		
Price per Share	Short 1 30 Call	Short 1 30 Put	Long 1 25 Put	Long 1 35 Call	Net
$40	$–915	$115	$– 95	$435	$–460
39	–815	115	– 95	335	–460
38	–715	115	– 95	235	–460
37	–615	115	– 95	135	–460
36	–515	115	– 95	35	–460
35	–415	115	– 95	– 65	–460
34	–315	115	– 95	– 65	–360
33	–215	115	– 95	– 65	–260
32	–115	115	– 95	– 65	–160
31	– 15	115	– 95	– 65	– 60
30	85	115	– 95	– 65	40
29	85	15	– 95	– 65	– 60
28	85	– 85	– 95	– 65	–160
27	85	–185	– 95	– 65	–260
26	85	–285	– 95	– 65	–360
25	85	–385	– 95	– 65	–460
24	85	–485	05	– 65	–460
23	85	–585	105	– 65	–460
22	85	–685	205	– 65	–460
21	85	–785	305	– 65	–460
20	85	–885	405	– 65	–460

This strategy is illustrated in Figure 5.10.

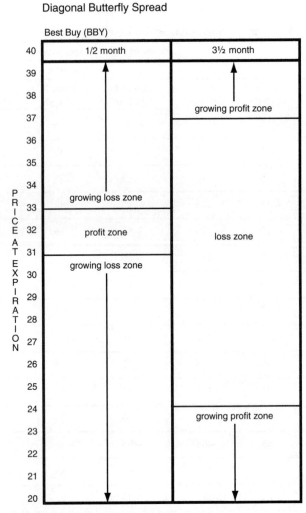

Figure 5.10   Diagonal Butterfly Spread, Best Buy

The outcome for this strategy cannot be viewed as a singular outcome because two different expiration dates are involved. The overall potential for loss is due primarily to increasing in-the-money status of the short options. However, remember that these expire in about two weeks, so the problem will largely evaporate as time value falls from both of these positions. It is conceivable that either or both the call and the put can be either closed at a small profit or allowed to expire worthless. After that has occurred, the longer expiration long call and put remain in effect. These can be allowed to ride or closed at small losses but adding to the overall profit of the position due to declining time value in the short contracts. The in-the-money short can also be rolled forward to avoid exercise.

> **Key Point:** When you have both a short call and a short put in the same strategy, one is likely to expire worthless and the other has to be closed at a profit due to time value decline, allowed to exercise, or rolled forward.

The purpose to all formations of straddles is to hedge the short risk in uncovered positions with long-side options. At the same time that the hedge protects you from unlimited risk, the short options are going to expire; thus, time value evaporates. When the short expiration occurs sooner than the long expiration, the spread in its many configurations is very advantageous. Even in those situations showing an overall loss, you cannot forget that the short positions contain time value that is going to go away; this creates the opportunity for profit even in the spread that appears programmed to result in a loss.

Like the spread, the straddle also combines various options in an interesting manner. While spreads are based on different strike prices, straddles use identical strikes for combinations of long call and put or short call and put. The next chapter takes a look at the many straddle opportunities focusing on puts.

6

PUT STRATEGIES FOR STRADDLES: PROFITS IN EITHER DIRECTION

I n the preceding chapter, examples of strategic uses of spreads demonstrated that you can put to work many varieties. You can reduce risks, hedge other positions, and leverage capital in many ways. The same argument applies equally to straddles.

A *straddle* is opening calls and puts together on the same underlying stock, with the same strike and the same expiration. The positions may be long or short. Although this basic definition applies to all straddles, the positions can be covered or uncovered, extended and altered, and adjusted to either increase or decrease levels of risk.

The Long Straddle

Many straddles come into being not as an initial strategy but as a development of a previously entered one. Just as puts can be purchased to protect paper profits, they can also be used to offset appreciated stock and to accompany a long call.

Long straddles—those in which both call and put positions are
purchased—create a maximum loss in the middle zones and profit
potential above and below. Because you have to overcome time value in
both option positions, you may require considerable movement in the
stock price to accomplish a profitable outcome. The problem for all
option buyers is just that: overcoming the time value premium before
expiration. Long straddles double up on this problem; however, the
potential for profit is found on both sides of price movement. It does
not matter whether the stock's value rises or falls, as long as the number
of points is enough to create a profit in one of the long positions.

Example of a long straddle: Consolidated Edison (market price $36.05
per share) had five-month options valued at the following levels:

strike	call	put
30	5.40	1.45
35	3.00	3.30
40	1.05	6.70

In this case, using five-month options is appropriate because, as long
positions, it will be necessary to allow time to pass for the stock's price
to move sufficiently to produce a profit in the position. Opening long
straddles at these price levels requires approximately seven points of
debit; this means the stock will need to move seven points either above
or below the strike to reach a breakeven point. For example, picking the
options closest to current price of the stock ($36.05), the 35 options
cost

35 call	−3.00
35 put	−3.30
Total debit	−6.30

The stock's value must fall below $28.70 or above $41.70 per share for
this long straddle to become profitable. The outcome at various prices
at expiration is summarized in Table 6.1.

Table 6.1   Consolidated Edison ($36.05)

Price	35 Call	35 Put	Net
$45	$ 700	$-330	$ 370
44	600	-330	270
43	500	-330	170
42	400	-330	70
41	300	-330	-30
40	200	-330	-130
39	100	-330	-230
38	0	-330	-330
37	-100	-330	-430
36	-200	-330	-530
35	-300	-330	-630
34	-300	-230	-530
33	-300	-130	-430
32	-300	- 30	-330
31	-300	70	-230
30	-300	170	-130
29	-300	270	-30
28	-300	370	70
27	-300	470	170
26	-300	570	270
25	-300	670	370

The maximum loss never exceeds the maximum debit, and potential profits rise point for point above and below the middle zone. However, the loss zone in this example is substantial, covering 13 points. The outcome is further illustrated in Figure 6.1.

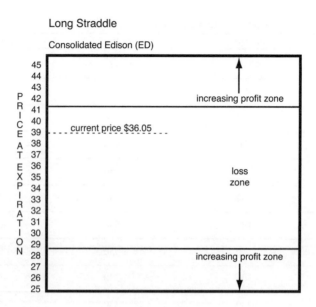

Long Straddle

Consolidated Edison (ED)

PRICE AT EXPIRATION

45
44
43
42 — increasing profit zone
41
40
39 — - - - current price $36.05 - - -
38
37
36
35 — loss zone
34
33
32
31
30
29
28 — increasing profit zone
27
26
25

Figure 6.1   Long Straddle, Consolidated Edison

The straddle does not necessarily remain open until expiration. It is likely that one side will be closed before the other, especially given the decline in time value that occurs when expiration approaches. So if you open a long straddle and the stock price rises, you will be likely to close the appreciated call when profits are available; and if the stock price falls enough for the put to become profitable, it would also make sense to close out that position. Looking at the straddle components individually, you need only about three points from the 35 strike to get to breakeven.

> **Key Point:** In a long straddle, profitable positions should be closed to take profits; if you wait too long, declining time value offsets the advantage.

As long as time value remains in either of the long positions, a profitable price could occur. It is even possible (but less likely) that the stock price during the coming five months could move in the money on first one option and then the other. This is against the odds, but within the realm of possibility.

The Short Straddle

The long straddle is problematic because it requires a very specific movement in the underlying stock to become profitable. That would consist of a strong movement in one direction, or movement adequate to create a profit in one option, followed by a reversal in the other direction. Long straddles may serve a purpose as part of a strategy to leverage capital for the long term (for example, buying LEAPS calls and puts in the belief that a two- or three-year price movement justifies that investment) or as a speculative move into the market when you expect a stock's price to be volatile in the near future. These problems are not the same for short straddles.

In a short straddle, you create a credit rather than a debit. This cushions your position so that, as long as the underlying stock remains in the middle price zone, the short straddle will be profitable. The risk, however, is the same as the risk for any short position: if the stock price moves enough in the money, one side of a short straddle will be exercised. Because this position includes both a call and a put, the risk is found in both a price increase and a price decrease.

An uncovered straddle write—one in which you do not own the underlying stock—contains two uncovered options: both a call and a put. This combines limited profit potential with unlimited risk potential. The credit you receive for selling an uncovered straddle provides a cushion against the risk, and exercise can be avoided by rolling a call forward and up, or rolling a put forward and down.

You have a distinct advantage in a short straddle. Unlike the long straddle, in which substantial price movement is required to offset time value, in a short position, time is on your side. Decline in time value makes profits more likely. Either side of the straddle can be closed profitably, often both sides. As long as the underlying stock's market value remains close to the strike price of the short straddle, time value will make both sides profitable before expiration, assuming early exercise does not occur. However, because early exercise is always a possibility, you have to be prepared for this in the event that it does occur.

Key Point: A common mistake is to assume that exercise will occur only on expiration day. Early exercise is always a possibility.

Example of market value above the strike: Sherwin-Williams (SHW) reported market value of $46.88 when the following options were available:

strike	call	put
40	10.00	3.20
45	6.50	6.00
50	4.10	8.90

It normally makes the most sense to pick a straddle as close as possible to current value of the underlying. However, depending on your outlook for the stock and belief about likely price direction, there may be instances in which you would pick a strike more points above or below market value, select a short spread as an alternative, or opt for a covered straddle rather than an uncovered straddle. Using the closest strikes, a short straddle would consist of selling two options:

Sell 45 call	6.50
Sell 45 put	6.00
Total credit	12.50

The profitable zone in this position will range 12.50 points above and below the straddle's strike. Above that, the short call represents unlimited risk; and below the price difference, the short put represents a risk (this is limited, of course, because the stock's price is unlikely to fall below tangible book value and certainly not beyond zero). So as long as the stock's price remains between 22.50 and 57.50, a limited profit will be earned. This is a considerable cushion, meaning that although the short straddle has greater market risk than the long straddle, profit is also far more likely.

The outcome at expiration for various price levels is summarized in Table 6.2.

Table 6.2 Sherwin-Williams ($46.88)

Price	45 Call	45 Put	Net
$75	$–2,350	$ 600	$–1,750
70	–1,850	600	–1,250
65	–1,350	600	–750
60	–850	600	–250
55	–350	600	250
50	150	600	750
45	650	600	1,250
40	650	100	750
35	650	–400	250
30	650	–900	–250
25	650	–1,400	–750
20	650	–1,900	–1,250
15	650	–2,400	–1,750

The short position at expiration could become quite expensive if the underlying price were to rise or fall beyond the safe and profitable range. Thus, you have to assume that one or the other of the short sides (or both) would be closed after time value had come out of the position. The short straddle is unlikely to remain open until expiration unless exercise of the in-the-money option would be considered desirable at that point. The outcome of the preceding example is illustrated in Figure 6.2.

> **Key Point:** After time value declines, it is wise to close out a short position to avoid exercise when in the money, or to roll forward to delay exercise.

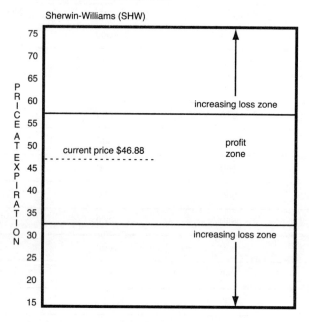

Uncovered Short Straddle

Sherwin-Williams (SHW)

PRICE AT EXPIRATION

current price $46.88

increasing loss zone

profit zone

increasing loss zone

Figure 6.2   Uncovered Short Straddle, Sherwin-Williams

A sensible approach to the short straddle would be to assume that exercise is acceptable, or to roll forward to avoid exercise. Given the wide range of profitable price points, this approach makes sense. However, remember that with the exception of the stock residing exactly at $45 per share, one of these positions is always in the money, so early exercise is a constant risk for the uncovered short straddle.

In comparison, the covered short straddle is not only less risky, but a relatively conservative play. To be entirely correct, the covered position refers only to the call side, which consists of a covered call (100 shares of stock held versus one covered call sold). The put side of the equation remains uncovered. However, downside risk is always finite, whereas uncovered upside risk in the example of a short call is potentially infinite. A stock's value cannot fall below zero and, for practical reasons, is unlikely to fall below its tangible book value. In writing a covered short straddle, the usual rules for profitable covered call writing apply. This means that the strike should be higher than the original basis in the stock. Otherwise, exercise creates a capital loss. When you ensure that if the call is exercised, a capital gain results, the outcome would not be undesirable.

Example: Union Pacific (UNP) was valued at $39.73 per share, when calls and puts were available for the following premium levels:

strike	call	put
35	7.80	5.50
40	5.80	8.30
45	3.20	9.70

In the case of the uncovered short straddle, it was considered desirable to select strikes as close as possible to current market value of the underlying. However, this is not necessarily the case for covered short straddles. In this example, the price per share is $39.73, which makes the 40 strike puts in the money. However, the 35 strike options are quite close in total value, and the put is nearly five points out of the money. As long as your basis in this stock is below the 35 strike, picking the 35 as a point for the short straddle makes sense, as long as exercise of the short call would be acceptable. This is far more likely because the stock at this point was nearly five points in the money. To compare the sale of two sets of options:

35 Strike

Call	7.80
Put	5.50
Total credit	13.30

40 Strike

Call	5.80
Put	8.30
Total credit	14.10

For a difference of only $80 in the overall credit, you can remove the put five points from likely exercise, while using the covered status of the call to insulate the position. In other words, exercise of the covered call would be more desirable than exercise of the uncovered put. The 13.30-point profit spread is a considerable range in this selection, as shown in Table 6.3.

Table 6.3   Union Pacific ($39.73)

Price	35 Call	35 Put	Net
$55	$–1,220	$ 550	$ – 670
50	–720	550	–170
45	–220	550	330
40	280	550	830
35	780	550	1,330
30	780	50	830
25	780	–450	330
20	780	–950	–170
15	780	–1,450	–670

This position contains a potentially substantial profit from the combined decline in time value for each of the short positions. If the stock price rises and the call is exercised, the growing loss does not affect the overall position. For example, if the stock rose to $55 and the $35 call is exercised, the 100 shares of stock would be called away at a profit. Meanwhile, the entire premium of $1,330 would be profit as well as the capital gain on the stock (remember, the covered call should be set up to create a gain in the event of exercise). While the potential profit from simply holding the stock would be greater than the combined exercise of the call and profit from the straddle, the chances of that outcome are remote. The covered short straddle produces profits as a certainty and for minimal risk.

> **Key Point:** Covered short straddles
> solve the problem of short call exercise,
> while generating attractive profits.

Whether stock prices rise or fall, exercise can be avoided on either side by rolling forward. Exercise may also be acceptable on the top side due to the covered call, or even on the bottom if the strike of $35 per share is considered reasonable. Upon exercise of the put, a subsequent covered short straddle could be entered, now with 200 shares and two each of short calls and puts. A decline in value may be recovered in this manner, even after a price decline in the stock. In the example, if the price were to decline as much as 13 points, the net credit on the straddle covers the loss.

The outcome is illustrated in Figure 6.3.

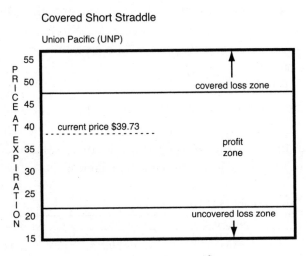

Figure 6.3   Covered Short Straddle, Union Pacific

Strangle Strategies

A variation of the straddle is the *strangle*. This is the combination of a call and a put with identical expiration dates but different strike prices. It is a hybrid strategy including features of both the spread and the straddle.

A long strangle usually includes identification of options that are out of the money. This reduces the initial debit for the position, but also increases the number of points of movement required in the underlying stock to create a profit. The advantage of the long strangle over the long straddle is that it is possible to select these positions; with a straddle, one or the other of the options is likely to be in the money.

An example of a long strangle: Abbott Labs (ABT) had market value of $47.70 per share when the following four-month options were available:

Buy 45 put	−2.10
Buy 50 call	−1.69
Total debit	−3.79

You can open the strangle for $379, which also means you need the stock's price to move nearly four points higher than the call strike or lower than the put strike, before the profit zone goes into effect. The outcome of this example is summarized in Table 6.4.

Table 6.4   Abbott Labs ($47.70)

Price	50 Call	45 Put	Total
$58	$631	$−210	$421
57	531	−210	321
56	431	−210	221
55	331	−210	121
54	231	−210	21
53	131	−210	−79
52	31	−210	−179
51	−69	−210	−279
50	−169	−210	−379
49	−169	−210	−379
48	−169	−210	−379
47	−169	−210	−379
46	−169	−210	−379

Table 6.4   Continued

Price	50 Call	45 Put	Total
45	−169	−210	−379
44	−169	−110	−279
43	−169	−10	−179
42	−169	90	− 79
41	−169	190	21
40	−169	290	121
39	−169	390	221
38	−169	490	321
37	−169	590	421

This outcome is also illustrated in Figure 6.4.

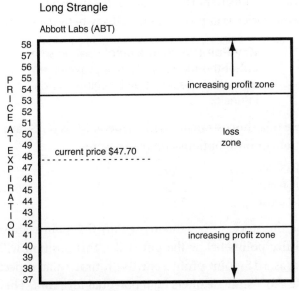

Figure 6.4   Long Strangle, Abbott Labs

The disadvantage in this strategy—the need to surpass a range of prices before profits are possible—also presupposes that the time value premium can be overcome during the time remaining before expiration.

This type of long strategy can also involve in-the-money options. The same stock had such options available, but the total debit would have been 8.30 (50 put at 4.30 and 45 call at 4.00). That requires a considerably higher loss zone totaling 16.60 points. The advantage in this position is that one or the other of these long positions will always be in the money, so the eight-point spread actually approximates a three-point risk level (assuming five points of intrinsic value at any price). So even though the debit is higher for an in-the-money long strangle, the comparison is not that far off. This also increases the likelihood that one side can be closed at a profit and the other left open, to later acquire intrinsic value higher than initial cost, one hopes.

The long strangle has some potential for speculating on price movement. In comparison, the short strangle offers some interesting strategic potential. It is normally created using out-of-the-money options. This maximizes the potential for profit because the nonintrinsic premium is 100 percent of the premium at the time the position is opened. You expect this to evaporate on an accelerated schedule as expiration approaches. The ideal short strangle is set up when the underlying stock's current price is approximately halfway between the two strikes.

> **Key Point:** A short strangle set up with out-of-the-money positions provides an advantage because all premium is non-intrinsic.

An example of a short strangle: With General Mills (GIS) at $53.82, the following four-month options and prices were

Sell 55 call	2.90
Sell 50 put	2.25
Total credit	5.15

As long as the stock price remains within five points above the call strike and five points below the put strike, this position will be profitable. That is a 15-point profit zone. With time value expected to fall rapidly, the short strangle offers high potential for profit. The risk associated with short options is offset by the profit zone size; exercise can be further avoided by rolling forward, or by closing one or both positions once the time value has declined enough. Any stock movement will take one of the positions further out of the money, so closing one side is a likely outcome. Closing both sides due to declining time value is the most likely occurrence. This position is summarized in Table 6.5.

Table 6.5   General Mills ($53.82)

Price	50 Call	45 Put	Total
$63	$–510	$225	$–285
62	–410	225	–185
61	–310	225	–85
60	–210	225	15
59	–110	225	115
58	–10	225	215
55	90	225	315
56	190	225	415
55	290	225	515
54	290	225	515
53	290	225	515
52	290	225	515
51	290	225	515
50	290	225	515
49	290	125	415
48	290	25	315
47	290	–75	215
46	290	–175	115
45	290	–275	15
44	290	–375	–85
43	290	–475	–185
42	290	–575	–285

This table demonstrates the sizable profit zone, including the maximum credit of $515 between the two option strikes. This outcome is illustrated in Figure 6.5.

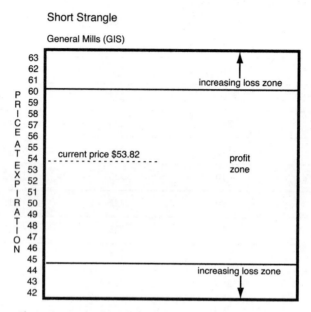

Figure 6.5   Short Strangle, General Mills

Because the profit zone is wider than the short straddle, the strangle appears to contain less risk. However, in the event of a rapid price movement in either direction, you could end up with a loss, resulting from needing to buy to close an in-the-money position. This situation can be avoided with a roll forward; however, a substantial price change poses a very real risk. If the stock does reach the high or low breakeven point, the strangle can be rolled into a straddle to mitigate the potential loss.

> **Key Point:** A short strangle with in-the-money options is higher risk even though it generates a higher initial credit for the position.

The strangle can also consist of in-the-money options to increase the initial credit. For example, General Mills also had a 50 call (at 5.70) and a 55 put (at 4.70) for a total credit premium of 10.40. The credit of over

$1,000 may be tempting, but in this more aggressive short strangle, one of the positions is always in the money. Therefore, the risk of exercise is unavoidable without closing a position or rolling forward. With a very short time to expiration, such a strategy is appealing because time value will disappear rapidly, and at least one side of the position is going to be worthless. However, the remaining in-the-money position has to be dealt with afterward.

Calendar Straddles

The straddle can be expanded to combine both long and short positions. The calendar straddle is actually two such strategies entered together. The usual structure involves selling the short-term straddle and then buying the longer-term one, creating the calendar effect. Time value in the near-term short positions will fall faster than the long-term ones, meaning that the overall position can be made profitable, leaving the possibility of the remaining long options open to be closed later or held in the hope of further profits.

An example of a calendar spread: Honeywell (HON) was valued at $26.86 and the following option positions were available:

One-month (short straddle)

27.50 call	1.45
27.50 put	2.10
Total credit	3.55

Three-month (long straddle)

27.50 call	−2.60
27.50 put	−3.13
Total debit	−5.73
Net debit	−2.18

For a net of $218, this position sets up the possibility of time value decline rapidly in the short positions, leaving the long positions in place. If the underlying stock were to rise, the short put (2.10) would expire worthless, covering nearly all the net debit. If the stock were to fall, the short call premium (1.45) would cover two-thirds of the net debit.

Key Point: The calendar strangle is a neutral position; with long options covering the shorts, profit comes from rapid decline in short time value, leaving additional profit potential in the remaining long positions.

The near-term short positions are covered by the long-term options of the same strike and, in fact, those can be used to offset exercise. The ideal position of the stock at expiration of the short positions would be exactly at the strike; however, it is more likely that one of the short options will be in the money and, if possible, may be closed at a small profit. The outcome of this position, overall, is summarized in Table 6.6. However, the overall outcome is not as critical as status of the short positions by expiration; because the calendar straddle is actually two offsetting positions, its advantage is found in the low cost and potential for profitable outcome, followed by additional profit potential in the outstanding long options.

Table 6.6   Honeywell ($26.86)

	1-month Short Straddle		3-month Long Straddle		
Price	27.50 Call	27.50 Put	27.50 Call	27.50 Put	Total
$35	$–605	$210	$490	$–313	$–218
34	–505	210	390	–313	–218
33	–405	210	290	–313	–218
32	–305	210	190	–313	–218
31	–205	210	90	–313	–218
30	–105	210	–10	–313	–218
29	–05	210	–110	–313	–218
28	95	210	–210	–313	–218
27	145	160	–260	–263	–218
26	145	60	–260	–163	–218
25	145	–40	–260	–63	–218
24	145	–140	–260	37	–218

Table 6.6   Continued

| | 1-month Short Straddle | | 3-month Long Straddle | | |
Price	27.50 Call	27.50 Put	27.50 Call	27.50 Put	Total
23	145	−240	−260	137	−218
22	145	−340	−260	237	−218
21	145	−440	−260	337	−218
20	145	−540	−260	437	−218
19	145	−640	−260	537	−218

The outcome, overall, at any price is always equal to the net debit, making the calendar straddle a neutral strategy. However, it is potentially profitable as well, assuming that the short positions are closed, exercised, or rolled before expiration. The whole idea is to close out the short positions due to rapidly declining time value premium and to leave the longer-term long options in place (or close them at some point) to create an overall profitable outcome. You only need to create receipts above $218 to accomplish this, and because shorts expire before longs, the short risk is not an issue (unless you close the long options before the short expirations occur). This position is illustrated in Figure 6.6.

This figure shows how each of these two straddles exists with its own profit or loss zones. However, because they coexist, the cover created between short and long offsets the loss position and sets up the neutrality. This provides potential for profits in one or both of the shorts as well as further profit potential in one of the long options.

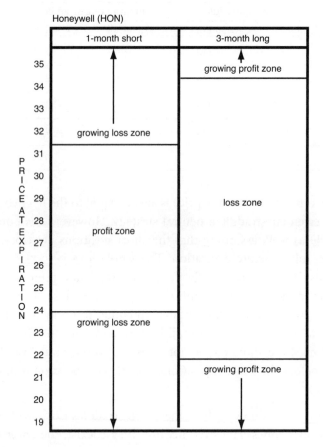

Figure 6.6 Calendar Straddle, Honeywell

To this point, spreads and straddles have been compared on a one-to-one option basis. So the positions have been set up to show what occurs when one option is opened long and another opened short, or one call and one put are utilized. Both strategic potential and hedging advantages can be modified by altering this balance and opening a ratio position. This occurs whenever one side contains more option contracts than the other. A range of ratio strategies is provided in the next chapter.

7

PUTS IN THE RATIO SPREAD: ALTERING THE BALANCE

A *ratio spread* refers to any strategy with two offsetting sides to a position, with one side weighted more heavily than the other. The best known of these is the ratio covered call, when more calls are sold than are covered. For example, if you own 300 shares of stock and sell four calls, this creates a 4-to-3 ratio spread. This can also be viewed as having three covered and one uncovered calls, but the ratio write does create advantages that reduce the uncovered call risk.

The premium received in the ratio write can be high enough to justify the ratio write. Because this adds downside protection, you can profit even if the short calls go in the money by either selling them or rolling one or more contracts forward to avoid or delay exercise. The position can also be protected by buying a call expiring later than the uncovered short position.

Another call-based method applies to the use of short calls versus later-expiring long calls. Writing more short positions also creates a call calendar ratio. Even though numerous ratio writes focus on calls, many put-based ratio spread strategies are also possible and should not be overlooked.

Ratio Put Spreads

The put-based ratio spread consists of more short puts than long puts. The longs expire at the same time and provide cover for a portion of the short position. For example, say you sell four puts and buy three at a higher strike. Abbott Labs (market price $47.70), for example, had two-month puts at the following levels:

45 puts	2.10
47.50 puts	2.86

A ratio spread of 3-to-2 is created if you sell three 45 puts and buy two 47.50 puts:

Sell three 45 puts @ 2.10	6.30
Buy two 47.50 puts @ 2.86	−5.72
Net credit	0.58

> **Key Point:** The ratio is defined as opening more short than long (or long than short) positions, to take advantage of declining time value. The short side is usually going to expire sooner.

Because these contracts expire at the same time, the ratio spread position presents partial coverage of the shorts by the longs. The stock was at $47.70, so all these options are out of the money. Even if the long put time value declines, the open contracts continue to provide coverage of the short 45 puts. If the stock falls below the lower strike, the uncovered portion (one put) can be rolled forward to avoid or defer exercise. The short risk based on current price level is only 2.12 points (current market price of $47.70 minus short strike of 45 = 2.70; and 2.70 minus net credit of 0.58 = 2.12). This position is summarized at various strike levels in Table 7.1.

Table 7.1 Abbott Labs ($47.70)

	Sell 3	Buy 2	
Price	45 Puts	47.50 Puts	Net
$50	$630	$−572	$58
49	630	−572	58

Table 7.1   Continued

	Sell 3	Buy 2	
Price	45 Puts	47.50 Puts	Net
48	630	−572	58
47	630	−472	158
46	630	−272	358
45	630	−72	558
44	330	128	458
43	30	328	358
42	−270	528	258
41	−570	728	158
40	−870	928	58
39	−1,170	1,128	−42
38	−1,470	1,328	−142
37	−1,770	1,528	−242

The growing net loss below the $40 per share level reflects the net difference in long and short positions; two of the short puts are covered by the long puts; so in reality, the loss is growing by a net of one point per drop in the stock's share price. This uncovered put can be closed, covered with another long put, or rolled forward. The position is illustrated in Figure 7.1.

The ratio put spread expands current income from the spread, while increasing risk. The fact that the long puts cover some of the short puts makes risk far less risky than it appears in a table or chart. The decline in time value of the short puts makes it likely that out-of-the-money positions will be closed at a profit or, if the stock's price remains above strike, allowed to expire worthless. If sold, the remaining long positions can also be sold for current value to increase profit from the ratio spread.

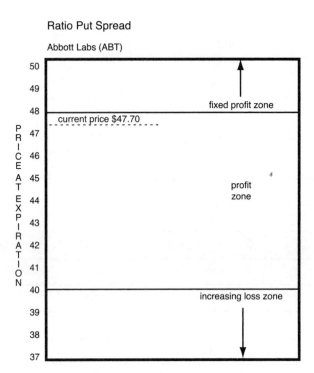

Figure 7.1   Ratio Put Spread, Abbott Labs

Ratio Put Calendar Spreads

The ratio put spread can be varied by time as well. The ratio calendar spread improves chances for short expiration while leaving longer-term long puts open. Because shorter-term short put time value will fall more rapidly than the longer-term long puts, the opportunity for a profitable outcome is favorable.

> **Key Point:** The ratio calendar spread involves not only a different number of long and short positions, but also different expiration dates.

For example, Honeywell (HON) was worth $26.86 when the following puts were available:

One-month 27.50 puts	2.10
Three-month 27.50 puts	3.13

You set up a ratio calendar spread by selling four of the one-month puts and buying three of the three-month puts:

Sell four one-month 27.50 puts   8.40
Buy three three-month puts   −9.39
Net debit   −0.99

Setting up this position costs $99; however, the short puts expire in one month. At the time of the position opening, all these puts were in the money by only 0.64. If the stock's market value remains at or above the 27.50 strike, the three short puts will expire worthless. If the stock declines below that level, three of the four short puts are covered by the longer-term long puts. The remaining position can be allowed to exercise, covered with another long put, or rolled forward to avoid exercise. The outcome of this strategy is summarized in Table 7.2.

Table 7.2   Honeywell ($26.86)

Price	Sell 4 27.50 Puts	Buy 3 27.50 Puts	Net
$33	$840	$−939	$−99
32	840	−939	−99
31	840	−939	−99
30	840	−939	−99
29	840	−939	−99
28	840	−939	−99
27	640	−789	−149
26	240	−489	−249
25	−160	−189	−349
24	−560	111	−449
23	−960	411	−549
22	−1,360	711	−649
21	−1,760	1,011	−749
20	−2,160	1,311	−849

The pattern looks similar to the one for the ratio put spread. However, in this calendar variety of the strategy, the shorts expire earlier than the longs. As a result, time value will decline more rapidly, reducing overall risk. After the short puts have expired, been closed, or rolled forward, the four long positions remain open. They can be closed to extend profits or allowed to ride in the hope of a further price decline in the underlying stock. In that case, the intrinsic value of the long puts in this example grows by four points for every one-point drop in the stock. The outcome of this position is also shown in Figure 7.2.

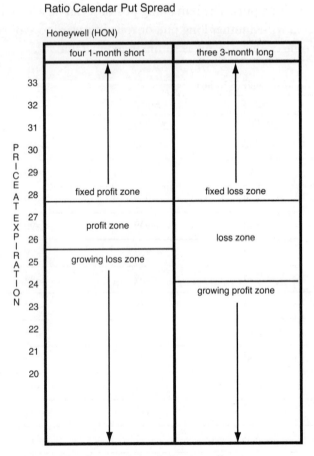

Figure 7.2   Ratio Calendar Put Spread, Honeywell

The Backspread (Reverse Ratio)

The backspread flips the relationship between long and short positions. In this variation, you buy more puts than you sell. This creates significantly greater profit opportunities while completely covering the short side risk. The long puts not only cover the shorts, but also provide additional opportunities if and when the stock's price declines. The long positions are bought at a higher strike than the shorts. In this way, an incrementally greater number of points will increase profitability on the long side. And if the price falls below the short strike, the long puts provide cover.

> **Key Point:** The backspread reverses the usual ratio, involving more long positions than short positions. This is advantageous if you expect a big price drop in the underling stock by long put expirations.

For example, SPDR Gold Shares (GLD) was at $87.58 per share when the following two-month puts were available:

85 put	3.40
88 put	5.00

The backspread includes many possible combinations of ratios. For example, a 3-to-2 may involve taking the following positions:

Buy three 85 puts @ 3.40	−10.20
Sell two 88 puts @ 5.00	10.00
Net debit	−0.20

This is practically a wash, although trading costs will increase the debit slightly. The great advantage here is that even with in-the-money short positions (in this case, the short puts are 0.42 in the money), the long puts have greater appreciation potential in the event the stock price falls. In the put backspread, the further the stock falls, the greater the profit. This occurs because the long side covers the short and exceeds coverage by an additional contract. If the stock price rises above the higher strike of 88 by expiration, the loss cannot exceed the original debit of 0.20. The outcome is shown at various prices in Table 7.3.

Table 7.3 SPDR Gold Shares ($87.68)

	Sell 2	Buy 3	
Price	88 Puts	85 Puts	Total
$90	$1,000	$–1,020	$–20
89	1,000	–1,020	–20
88	1,000	–1,020	–20
87	800	–1,020	–220
86	600	–1,020	–420
85	400	–1,020	–620
84	200	–720	–520
83	0	–420	–420
82	–200	–120	–320
81	–400	180	–220
80	–600	480	–120
79	–800	780	–20
78	–1,000	1,080	80
77	–1,200	1,380	180
76	–1,400	1,680	280
75	–1,600	1,980	380
74	–1,800	2,280	480
73	–2,000	2,580	580
72	–2,200	2,880	680

This strategy is desirable because it fixed maximum loss at the net debit, which in this case is minimal. Remember also that the short positions can be closed after time value declines, enabling you to profit from the short side while eliminating exercise risk, and the remaining long puts can be sold or closed. This strategy is illustrated in Figure 7.3.

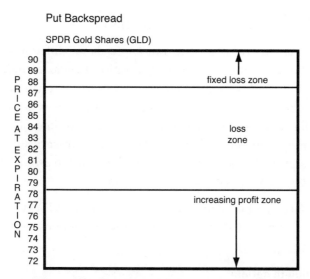

Put Backspread

SPDR Gold Shares (GLD)

Figure 7.3   Put Backspread, SPDR Gold Shares

It is possible to create a backspread with a net credit, but ultimately the goal should be to open a position for very little net cost or benefit; the real potential lies in exploiting a declining time value and also profiting from long positions in either remaining time value premium or an increase in intrinsic value premium. Early exercise is always a possibility in a strategy like this, where long puts provide cover for shorts. The three-point difference between strikes represents a realistic risk in this case, even with the short positions only slightly in the money. As long as the underlying stock's price remains in the current proximity to strike, time value will occur. And with only two months remaining until expiration, the time value should fall rapidly.

> **Key Point:** The risk of early exercise
> should never be overlooked; however,
> with the ratio approach, the exposure is
> limited to the uncovered short positions.

If the possibility of early exercise becomes an increasing concern due to a declining stock price, the short puts can also be rolled forward to defer exercise (or forward and down to reduce the cost of exercise). In this issue, puts were available in one-point increments, making rolling far more flexible than stocks with 5-point or even 2.5-point strike increments.

Ratio Calendar Combinations

What happens if you open two ratio spreads on different expiration dates at the same time? This creates a ratio calendar combination. A longer-term spread is opened long versus a shorter-expiring short position. The creation of a ratio favoring the short side is advantageous. These will expire sooner, limiting risk exposure. As time value declines more rapidly in the shorts than in the longs, the earlier positions can be closed at a profit, allowed to expire, rolled forward to avoid exercise, or subsequently covered with new long positions.

An example of a ratio calendar combination: Boeing (BA) was priced at $33.75 per share. At that time, the following options positions and prices were reported:

2-month options:

strike	calls	puts
30	5.29	1.40
35	2.20	3.20

5-month options:

strike	calls	puts
30	6.40	2.85
35	3.30	3.90

Generally speaking, a higher number of contracts opened at the same time would be considered to contain greater risk than a lower number. With ratio strategies, the opposite is true. A ratio position can consist of any weighting you desire. A 2-to-1 is higher risk than a 3-to-2 or a 4-to-3 because the relative uncovered portion is greater in the lower ratios:

ratio	uncovered
2-to-1	50%
3-to-2	33%
4-to-3	25%

For the Boeing example, a ratio calendar combination can consist of any mix among these options. The following example is based on a two-month spread opened short with four out-of-the-money positions and the five-month spread opened long with three positions:

2-month:

Sell four 30 calls @ 5.29	21.16
Sell four 35 puts @ 3.20	12.80

5-month:

Buy three 30 calls @ 6.40	−19.20
Buy three 35 puts @ 3.90	−11.70
Net credit	3.06

Although the level of cost is high for each of these four positions, the overall net is only a credit of $306. The outcome is also adjusted by the fact that the short positions expire in two months, whereas the long positions have five months remaining. And because all these options are out of the money, time value is going to evaporate quickly over the next two months for the shorts. These can be closed at a profit after time value has declined, left to expire worthless (one side will remain out of the money at expiration), or rolled forward to avoid exercise (the other short side will be in the money at expiration).

> **Key Point:** When all the options are out of the money, you have a distinct advantage with the short puts. The likelihood of being able to close at a profit or wait out expiration is far better than if you use in-the-money puts.

The net exposure is only a single contract because the long positions cover the shorts; the maximum risk occurs if the underlying stock's market value moves significantly in either direction. The most advantageous outcome, given time value of the shorts, is for the stock price to remain between the 30 and 35 strikes until expiration. The outcome of this strategy is shown in Table 7.4.

Table 7.4   Boeing ($33.75)

	2-month Short Spread		5-month Long Spread		
	Sell 4	Sell 4	Buy 3	Buy 3	
Price	30 Calls	5 Puts	30 Calls	35 Puts	Total
$60	$–9,884	1,280	7,920	$–1,170	$–1,854
55	–7,884	1,280	6,420	–1,170	–1,354
50	–5,884	1,280	4,920	–1,170	–854
45	–3,884	1,280	3,420	–1,170	–354
40	–1,884	1,280	1,920	–1,170	146
35	116	1,280	–420	–1,170	–194
30	2,116	–720	–1,920	330	–194
25	2,116	–2,720	–1,920	1,830	–694
20	2,116	–4,720	–1,920	3,330	–1,194
15	2,116	–6,720	–1,920	4,830	–1,694
10	2,116	–8,720	–1,920	6,330	–2,194

The total losses reflected on the table are provided only to show the overall impact of the spreads; however, because the short positions expire earlier than the long positions, the ratio calendar combination actually contains two separate profit and loss zones. The short positions are not entirely at risk either, due to the coverage by longs of all but a single position. In the event of early exercise of either call or put, the long positions provide cover. One additional advantage to the multiple-contract ratio is that early exercise for all the short positions is highly unlikely. In this case, with four short contracts, it is possible to have one or two exercised in this manner, but experiencing early exercise for all four is only a remote possibility. The strategy is further illustrated in Figure 7.4.

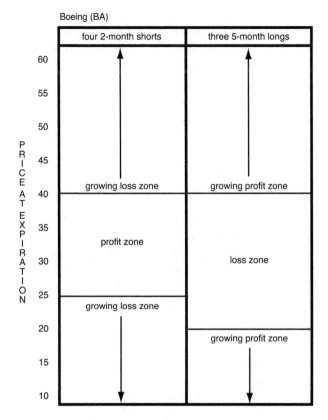

Figure 7.4   Ratio Calendar Combination, Boeing

The ratio calendar combination, even with fewer outstanding contracts, should be entered only if margin requirements can be easily met
from current levels of cash and securities in your brokerage account.
The position can become profitable as long as price movement is not
too extreme; for this reason, advanced strategies with many short positions should be avoided on highly volatile issues. In such cases, early
exercise can turn a "sure thing" profit into an unexpected loss very
quickly. However, the ratio calendar combination is an excellent strategy to take advantage of rapid decline in time value. When it is properly
structured, you can produce a no-cost long position after shorts are
closed and/or expired. When this occurs, one side of the remaining long
positions will always be in the money, so the chances for further profits

are good. Even if the long positions are simply closed for their current value after the shorts have been dealt with, the overall outcome of the position will be profitable. The initial credit, plus profits from the closing of shorts and longs, can make the position a good cash generator. Having a ratio position open with numerous offsetting short and long options expands the potential for exploiting the short-term volatility of the underlying stock.

The Diagonal Backspread

The *backspread* is defined as a spread in which long positions outnumber the short. If you set this up on a diagonal, with varying expirations, it creates a diagonal backspread. For example, Caterpillar (CAT) was at $27.47 when the following options and premiums were listed:

2-month options:

strike	calls	puts
27	2.14	2.02
28	1.58	2.61

3-month options:

strike	calls	puts
27	2.62	2.89
28	2.25	3.25

A diagonal backspread contains three attributes. First, you open more long than short positions; second, the shorts expire earlier than the longs. Third, the shorts are opened with higher strikes than the longs. For example:

Sell one 2-month 28 put	2.61
Buy two 3-month 27 puts @ 3.25	−6.50
Net debit	−3.89

Table 7.5 summarizes the outcome of this strategy.

Table 7.5   Caterpillar ($27.47)

	Sell 1	Buy 2	
	2-month	3-month	
Price	28 Puts	27 Puts	Total
$32	$261	$-650	$-389
31	261	-650	-389
30	261	-650	-389
29	261	-650	-389
28	261	-650	-389
27	161	-650	-489
26	61	-450	-389
25	-39	-250	-289
24	-139	-50	-189
23	-239	150	-89
22	-339	350	11
21	-439	550	111
20	-539	750	211
19	-639	950	311

Key Point: The three attributes in the diagonal backspread are more long puts than short, earlier short expiration, and higher strikes in the short than in the long puts.

This strategy, like many other ratio spreads, involves sooner-expiring short positions. Thus, as time value declines, these can be closed at a profit or, if the stock remains above the strike, allowed to expire worthless. The long positions remain open longer and can be either kept open hoping for a decline in the underlying, or closed at any time after the short expiration date. Because long positions outnumber and outlast shorts, the maximum risk in this position is the initial debit of $389.

The most advantageous outcome is for the underlying to remain at or above the short strike until expiration and to then decline. The outcome of this is illustrated in Figure 7.5.

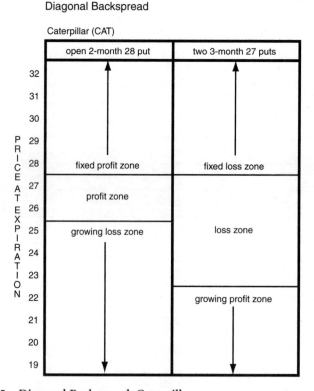

Figure 7.5 Diagonal Backspread, Caterpillar

The diagonal backspread, because it sets up a debit in this example, is advantageous only if you expect the stock price to decline after expiration of the short puts. (A similar assumption applies to call-based diagonal backspreads when your expectation is that the price will rise after expiration of the short call positions.) If this is not certain, a simple calendar spread or a ratio spread makes more sense and will create a net credit and greater profit potential.

Short Ratio Puts

A final type of ratio applies to a hedging strategy when you have shorted stock. Just as a short call is covered by 100 shares of long stock, a short put has a similar effect when you are short 100 shares of stock, although the benefit is limited. You short stock when you expect it to fall; however, if it rises, a short put declines in value and offsets the net loss in the stock. If you sell a 35 put for 4.50 when you short the stock at $35 per share, for example, you gain protection up to a rise in the stock to $39.50 per share. If the stock rises above that level, losses begin to accrue.

This problem can be mitigated by using a short put ratio strategy. For example, in a 2-to-1 short put, you would sell two puts against 100 short shares. Or in a 3-to-2, you sell three puts against 200 shares sold.

For example, Molson Coors Brewing (TAP) was selling for $33.14 per share. If you had shorted 200 shares of this stock when it was at $35 per share, you could hedge against potential losses in the event the stock were to rise. So you sell three 35 puts at 4.50 and receive $1,350. The outcome at various prices for this strategy is shown in Table 7.6.

Table 7.6 Molson Coors Brewing ($33.14)

Price	Short 200 Shares	Sell 3 35 Puts	Total
$45	$–2,000	$1,350	$–650
44	–1,800	1,350	–450
43	–1,600	1,350	–250
42	–1,400	1,350	–50
41	–1,200	1,350	150
40	–1,000	1,350	350
39	–800	1,350	550
38	–600	1,350	750
37	–400	1,350	950
36	–200	1,350	1,150

Table 7.6 Continued

Price	Short 200 Shares	Sell 3 35 Puts	Total
35	0	1,350	1,150
34	200	1,050	1,150
33	400	750	1,150
32	600	450	1,050
31	800	150	950
30	1,000	−150	850
29	1,200	−450	750
28	1,400	−750	650
27	1,600	−1,050	550
26	1,800	−1,350	450
25	2,000	−1,650	350
24	2,200	−1,950	250
23	2,400	−2,250	150
22	2,600	−2,550	50
21	2,800	−2,850	−50
20	3,000	−3,150	−150
19	3,200	−3,450	−250

Because the credit you receive from selling the puts is fixed, this ratio protects the short only to a degree. The hedging properties decline as the stock's price rises higher. On the downside, the profit on the short stock is offset by the losses on the higher number of short puts. The advantage to this strategy is that it creates a profit zone of considerable breadth, 20 points in all.

Key Point: The short ratio put strategy removes most of the risk from the short stock *and* from the short put positions. The expanded profit zone gives you time to close out the entire strategy without a loss, regardless of the price direction.

If the stock's price began to rise, it would make sense to close both sides (short stock and short puts) before the overall profitability disappeared. Compared to simply selling stock, the short put ratio provides a greater upside profit zone (six points in the example), but it also erodes downside profits for the short stock. The strategy is summarized in Figure 7.6.

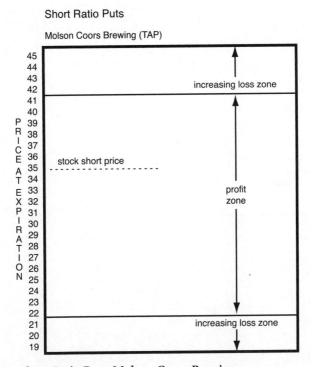

Figure 7.6   Short Ratio Puts, Molson Coors Brewing

The short stock strategy involves specific market risks. The short ratio puts strategy hedges the market risk by expanding the profit zone and softening the effects of losses. Because the profit range is expanded, this also makes it easier to shut down the position as loss zones approach, either on the upside or the downside.

The many ratio strategies demonstrate how profits can be increased without adding undue market risk or how profits can be limited in exchange for reducing market risks. Another method for accomplishing the same idea is the use of put-based synthetic strategies. These are explained in the next chapter.

8

PUTS AS PART OF SYNTHETIC STRATEGIES: PLAYING STOCKS WITHOUT THE RISK

Anyone who hesitates to buy stock in a volatile market may want to consider setting up *synthetic* strategies as an alternative. A synthetic is any position that duplicates the performance of stock, without the market risk or even the requirement to purchase shares.

A synthetic position performs like the stock position it imitates. This applies to either long or short stock.

Synthetic Stock Strategies

It is entirely possible to leverage your capital to the extreme with synthetic positions. Synthetic long stock is an options position that very closely approximates movement in the stock, but for practically no cost, or in some cases even a credit. The outcome of the option position relies on the proximity between strike prices and current value of the stock. To set up a synthetic long stock position, you buy a call and sell a put at the same strike.

Key Point: A synthetic position is advantageous because the net cost is near zero. But it enables you to create a position that acts the same as ownership of 100 shares.

For example, in the case of Caterpillar (market value $27.47), the three-month 27 call and put were valued closely; a synthetic long stock position is constructed using these options:

Buy one 27 call	−2.62
Sell one 27 put	2.89
Net credit	0.27

The small net credit would probably be offset by trading costs, making this a zero-gain, zero-loss transaction. Because the cost is virtually zero, you accomplish an equivalent position to owning 100 shares. This is demonstrated in the comparison in Table 8.1.

Table 8.1   Caterpillar ($27.47)

Stock		Option Positions		
Price	Profit	Long Call	Short Put	Net
$35	$ 800	$ 538	$ 289	$ 827
34	700	438	289	727
33	600	338	289	627
32	500	238	289	527
31	400	138	289	427
30	300	38	289	327
29	200	−62	289	227
28	100	−162	289	127
27	0	−262	289	27
26	−100	−262	189	−73
25	−200	−262	89	−173
24	−300	−262	−11	−273
23	−400	−262	−111	−373

Table 8.1 Continued

| Stock | | Option Positions | | |
Price	Profit	Long Call	Short Put	Net
22	−500	−262	−211	−473
21	−600	−262	−311	−573
20	−700	−262	−411	−673

This synthetic position follows profit and loss on the stock very closely. If the choice is between buying 100 shares of stock and paying out more than $2,700, or opening a synthetic long stock position for zero investment, this choice makes sense. One major difference is that no dividends will be earned with the synthetic long position (in the case of CAT, dividend yield was about 6 percent). As with all options comparisons, dividends should never be left out of the comparison; however, this demonstrates that there is an alternative to placing a large sum of capital at risk to acquire shares of stock.

This example raises yet another issue. The same situation could be accomplished with 10 long calls and short puts, thus controlling 1,000 shares of stock instead of 100. The profit and loss will also be 10 times more, and margin requirements would be higher as well. The point, however, is that synthetic strategies enable you to duplicate the profit opportunities (while also being exposed to the same risks) as buying shares of stock.

> **Key Point:** You can expand a synthetic position with no additional increase in the net cost; however, this also increases profit potential and market risk, as well as margin requirements.

The synthetic long stock position can be further protected by purchasing one insurance put per synthetic position. Just as long stock positions are protected in this manner, the insurance put offsets or limits the potential loss. However, if downside risk is a big concern, the alternative is to simply buy one long call and accept the time value call risk in place of the synthetic duplication of price movement with its own profit and loss.

You can also create a synthetic short stock position. For many people, the costs and risks of shorting stock are not acceptable; however, you can duplicate the price movement of stock without margin interest, and for little or no initial cost. A synthetic short sale of stock is accomplished by selling a call and buying a put at the same strike.

For example, Abbott Labs (ABT) stock was priced at $47.70 when the following two-month options could be used to create a synthetic short sale:

Sell one 47.50 strike call	2.75
Buy one 47.50 strike put	-2.86
Net debit	- 0.11

For a debit of only $11, you accomplish price movement identical to selling 100 shares of the underlying. The comparative outcome of this synthetic short sale is summarized in Table 8.2.

Table 8.2   Abbott Labs ($47.70)

Stock		Option Positions		
Price	Profit	Short Call	Long Put	Net
$54	$–650	$–375	$–286	$–661
53	–550	–275	–286	–561
52	–450	–175	–286	–461
51	–350	–75	–286	–361
50	–250	25	–286	–261
49	–150	125	–286	–161
48	–50	225	–286	–61
47	50	275	–236	39
46	150	275	–136	139
45	250	275	–36	239
44	350	275	64	339
43	450	275	164	439
42	550	275	264	539

Table 8.2   Continued

| Stock | | Option Positions | | |
Price	Profit	Short Call	Long Put	Net
41	650	275	364	639
40	750	275	464	739

Just as the synthetic long stock strategy tracked stock price movement, the synthetic short stock accomplishes the same outcome. If your choice comes down to shorting stock or opening a synthetic short position, the latter costs less and duplicates the same risks. If you are sensitive to upside loss risk, you can later purchase a call to reduce or eliminate the declining net profit. This "insurance call" becomes the equivalent of long-side insurance put, but on the short side.

> **Key Point:** Just as the insurance put protects long position profits, the insurance call is used to protect profits and to freeze losses for shorted stock.

Synthetic Strike Splits

The synthetic stock position can be varied by employing different strike prices. A split strike approach can be based on selecting out-of-the-money calls and puts rather than options close to the money.

For example, to create a synthetic long position on Boeing (BA) when its price was $33.75, you could open the following positions:

Buy one five-month 35 call	−3.30
Sell one five-month 30 put	2.85
Net debit	−0.45

Your net cost of $45 sets up a synthetic position creating the synthetic long stock position. The outcome compared to the stock's price movement from the $34 price level (the closest round number value) is shown in Table 8.3.

Table 8.3 Boeing ($33.75)

Stock Price	Profit	Option Positions Long Call	Short Put	Net
$45	$1,100	$ 670	$ 285	$ 955
44	1,000	570	285	855
43	900	470	285	755
42	800	370	285	655
41	700	270	285	555
40	600	170	285	455
39	500	70	285	355
38	400	−30	285	255
37	300	−130	285	155
36	200	−230	285	55
35	100	−330	285	−45
34	0	−330	285	−45
33	−100	−330	285	−45
32	−200	−330	285	−45
31	−300	−330	285	−45
30	−400	−330	285	−45
29	−500	−330	185	−145
28	−600	−330	85	−245
27	−700	−330	−15	−345
26	−800	−330	−115	−445
25	−900	−330	−215	−545

Because the strikes are varied, the synthetic nature of this strategy is altered. It reduces the higher price tracking slightly but also reduces the lower-price losses. This is due to the five-point differences in the strikes as well as the basis in the stock that is in between the two strikes. The mid-range loss of $45 maximum between the two strike price levels is equal to the cost of the synthetic position.

> **Key Point:** Changing the strikes within a synthetic strategy also alters the price tracking nature of the synthetic position.

The Synthetic Put

Shorting stock contains unlimited risk, at least in theory. A stock's value can rise indefinitely so that it is a high-risk strategy. The risk is reduced to a fixed amount with a synthetic put (also called the protected short sale).

This strategy is most likely to be opened after stock has been sold. When you buy one call, the potential maximum loss is fixed at the strike of the call, plus the cost of buying the call. Each point rise in the stock represents a loss, but each in-the-money point rise in the long call offsets that loss. Because the short stock position becomes profitable if prices fall, the combined position to the downside approximates the price action of a put; thus, it is called a *synthetic put*. Buying the call to mitigate loss is preferable in many instances to the more common reaction—covering the short sale. This creates a loss and is a rational decision when prices are rising quickly, but the synthetic put gives you a second way to manage risk and curtail losses.

For example, an investor shorted 100 shares of Union Pacific (UNP) at $37 per share; the current price is $39.73. Because the investor fears that the price might rise further, his first instinct is to close the short and limit the loss to the nearly three points; however, a synthetic put also limits the loss. Instead of closing the position, the investor buys a five-month 40 put for 5.80. This limits the potential loss. If the stock's price rises before expiration, the call's intrinsic value offsets the loss point for point; if the stock's price falls, the gain in the short stock eventually offsets the cost of the call. The position at various price levels is summarized in Table 8.4.

Table 8.4   Union Pacific ($39.73)

Stock Price	Profit	40 Call	Net
$48	$–1,100	$ 220	$ –880
47	–1,000	120	–880
46	–900	20	–880
45	–800	– 80	–880
44	–700	– 180	–880
43	–600	– 280	–880
42	–500	– 380	–880
41	–400	– 480	–880
40	–300	– 580	–880
39	–200	– 580	–780
38	–100	– 580	–680
37	0	– 580	–580
36	100	– 580	–480
35	200	– 580	–380
34	300	– 580	–280
33	400	– 580	–180
32	500	– 580	– 80
31	600	– 580	20
30	700	– 580	120
29	800	– 580	220
28	900	– 580	320

In this situation, the maximum loss is fixed at the price of the call plus the price difference between basis in the short stock ($37) and the call's strike (40). However, if the stock's price does decline, a growing profit zone develops at the $31 per share price level. This is a defensive strategy for anyone who has shorted stock and who continues to believe in its downside trend, but who also wants to fix the maximum loss. It is a method to freeze the maximum loss while waiting out the development of that trend. This strategy is illustrated in Figure 8.1.

> **Key Point:** You should use a synthetic put when you want to keep shorted stock open, but you have become concerned with upside risk. This approach requires acceptance of loss and requires greater downside movement to create a profit.

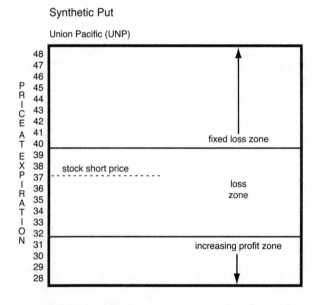

Synthetic Put

Union Pacific (UNP)

Figure 8.1   Synthetic Put, Union Pacific

The best call to buy to create this strategy is one close to the money. If you pick a call out of the money, it sets the maximum loss at a higher level; and if you pick a call in the money, the cost of the call also increases the loss level. The example of the UNP call at 5.80 is on the high side because even though it is out of the money, there are five months until expiration. In picking the right call, balancing cost with proximity between strike and current value is one problem; you also have to balance cost versus time. If time is short, the cost is lower but protection is similarly limited.

Synthetic strategies help avoid market risk in especially volatile markets. The next chapter expands on this idea. It examines the use of puts in contrary price trends (bear market rallies and bull market declines, for example) and demonstrates how particular technical signals can be used to anticipate changes in trends.

9

PUTS IN CONTRARY PRICE RUN-UPS: SAFE COUNTER-PLAYS DURING BEAR MARKETS

I f you have studied options, you already know that premium levels vary widely. The degree of volatility in a particular stock directly affects option premiums as a reflection of market risk. It is a common mistake to focus on the higher price potential in strategies such as covered calls and other shorts, but the higher premium also indicates higher volatility and market risk.

Making assumptions about price direction of a stock is a challenging task by itself. When you add the second requirement, estimating how volatile the stock is going to be, the options challenge becomes even greater. In a review of premium values, the two best-known types of value are predictable and well understood. Intrinsic value is tied specifically to the in-the-money status of an option and is equal to the number of points of stock value. If a 35 put is worth 4 and the stock is at $33 per share, the premium contains two points of intrinsic value. Time value premium is also a fairly predictable feature of the option. Its decline accelerates as expiration approaches, ending up at zero on expiration day when no time remains.

Option Valuation and Volatility

Many studies of option premium do not make a distinction between time and extrinsic value. The overall nonintrinsic value is described as "time value" but actually includes variation caused by a combination of time to expiration and volatility in the underlying stock. Separating these out clarifies the analysis. Time value is predictable and specific. It is going to decline at a known rate that is quite slow with many months to expiration and that accelerates as that date draws near. Extrinsic value is more complex. It varies based on volatility, accompanied by some adjustment to intrinsic value based on time itself.

> **Key Point:** Time value premium as commonly defined includes a third element, *extrinsic* value, which may also be called volatility premium.

For example, a LEAPS put with more than two years to go until expiration may act in what appears to be a puzzling manner. If the put is in the money and the underlying falls three points, you would expect the put to rise three points. This would occur if expiration were quite close, but the further away expiration is, the less responsive the put's premium will be. For example, the premium might rise only two points in response to a three-point decline in the stock. Why is this?

The time value does not adjust itself in this manner, and intrinsic value is quite specific as well. So the three-point in-the-money change consists of two parts. First, intrinsic value does increase by three points. Second, extrinsic value offsets that increase with a one-point decline. This reflects the fact that with so long to go until expiration, the true valuation of the put's premium cannot be known, so the overall premium is adjusted to reflect the uncertainty of the long-term remaining life of the option. In fact, all the uncertainty lies in the extrinsic value. The overall time decay in an option is not consistent among options on different underlying stocks because the market risk (volatility) varies considerably. So even when the time to expiration is identical, the degree of in-the-money premium is the same, and all other characteristics of the option are the same or similar, the reaction of premium to a change in the underlying price is not going to be the same. If intrinsic and time value were the only features to consider, this would not be the case;

options would all behave in the same manner. The variable is in the volatility of the underlying stock.

The unresponsiveness of long-term options to price movement in the underlying is even more pronounced when the option is out of the money. Here again, time value itself has not changed and, although you do not expect a point-for-point change in option premium out of the money, the degree of change is often quite small. The further away from expiration, the less response you should expect to see in the option's out-of-the-money premium.

> **Key Point:** When an option is a long
> way from expiration, out-of-the-money
> reaction to movement in the underlying
> stock is going to be quite low.

These realities are all in play when you study the volatility of options. Given the known decline in time value (if it could be isolated) as well as the specific attribute of intrinsic value (and its point-for-point change with the underlying), the remaining adjustments in premium are due to volatility. You see this in both directions. A stock's price change may cause little or no reaction in long-term options. Equally possible, the intrinsic change in option premium may cause *more* point movement than intrinsic value causes, indicating that in fact, a sentiment favoring more such movement is causing the adjustment to extrinsic value. So a put's value could exceed intrinsic value movement if there is a sentiment that the downward movement could be severe in the future, just as much as a call's premium could change in the opposite direction if sentiment is more optimistic.

The extrinsic value has a corner on the unknown element of option valuation. This is where the most interesting aspects of options pricing occur. In spite of many attempts to mathematically quantify option valuation, the fact remains that no one can specifically state how or why option valuation moves as it does.

> **Key Point:** All the uncertainties of
> option pricing reside in extrinsic value;
> both time value and intrinsic value are
> predictable and specific.

To some traders, this uncertainty is troubling news. It is only human to cry out for certainty even though it is never possible—just as a day trader or even a long-term value investor wants to *know* whether a stock's price is going to move up or down. But just as this is never certain, option valuation is not either. There is great emphasis in the study of time value and time decay as the most important variable in option strategies. But the point to remember is that time decay is both predictable and quantifiable. It can be studied and assigned specific value as expiration approaches. Within a week or less to expiration, intrinsic value works nearly alone, with very little time or extrinsic value in play. This is the timing when pure analysis is possible. The out weeks and months preceding the near-expiration timing contain increasingly higher uncertainty. The extension of uncertainty reflects volatility in the underlying and is the realm of the unknown and unpredictable.

These observations have to affect virtually all strategies and applications. In preceding chapters, the outcomes of each strategy were shown. This is important for comparative purposes, if only to show a "pure" analysis of a strategy's maximum profit or loss zones. In practice, any position is likely to be closed early to take profits or to cut losses; short positions may be subsequently covered or rolled forward to avoid exercise; and even though exercise is not inevitable, some positions may be entered to accept exercise. (For example, a covered call is one way to take a capital gain as well as option income, as opposed to simply selling shares of stock.)

The point is that even with the at-expiration analysis, strategic outcomes are going to vary considerably due to changes in extrinsic value. Unexpected profitable opportunities are likely to arise and, for the same reasons, unexpected risk of losses may appear in any position. So in entering any position, options traders invariably become volatility traders as well.

Volatility Trading

Option premium is assumed to follow a program based on time value and on proximity between current value of the underlying and the strike of the option. For example, it is true that as the proximity narrows, option premium becomes more responsive to movement in the underlying. This does not mean that time value has somehow changed; it does tell you that the implied volatility of the option has adjusted. This is the option's own volatility, distinguished from the market risk (volatility) of the underlying itself. One of many mathematical formulae can be applied to identify a theoretical value for an option. The Black-Scholes Model is the best-known of these, but it is also flawed in a few ways. Most of all, any model is going to be at variance between assignment of what the price should be and what it is in the current market. So implied volatility (which is a forward-looking estimate of option value) is quite different from a stock's historical volatility, which is specific and based on previous price range, especially in comparison to the market as a whole.

> **Key Point:** Because implied volatility is forward-looking, it is only an estimate. In highly volatile markets, its reliability will be predictably low.

Awareness of volatility had led to the development of many trading systems. This technical trend is made practical with the Internet, where even complex financial models can be calculated very quickly. An options trader who focuses on volatility spikes rather than on price believes that identifying volatility tops and bottoms is easier than trying to identify price tops and bottoms. This is an intriguing possibility, but for most options traders, short-term historical volatility in the underlying is more useful (at least in quantifying market risk) than trying to anticipate implied volatility. The unknown aspects, especially in exceptionally volatile stock markets, make this too uncertain. Given the trend in markets to be highly volatile (due to rapid trading systems online, global market penetration, evolution of Exchange Traded Funds (ETFs) in the institutional world, and more than anything, volume of trading in indices), traditional implied volatility studies are less reliable today than in the past. Academia continues to love Black-Scholes with its certainty and mathematical conclusiveness, but in the real world of options strategies, implied volatility is only one tool among many.

In making the distinction between historical and implied volatility, it is most important to recognize that one is historical and the other forward looking. Historical volatility is simply the record of a stock's trading range and price swings measured on a percentage basis. It is the degree of deviation in price from the average price of the market. It is usually calculated as *beta*, or the tendency of a stock's price to react to a price direction in the market. When a stock's beta is 1, it means the price is most likely to track the market trend. If beta is less than 1, this means it is less responsive to market price trends; and if the stock's beta is more than 1, it tends to move more strongly than the market in general. For example, a beta of 1.1 tells you that stock is likely to be 10 percent more volatile than the market in general.

Implied volatility applies to options rather than to the underlying. It is the calculated tendency of an option to increase or decrease in value in relation to movement in the underlying stock. Because it is a calculation estimating the future, it is not a specific concept. Even comparisons between options on different stocks cannot be used solely to quantify option volatility (because every stock is different and also because implied volatility is only an estimate), so as a comparative tool, implied volatility has limited value.

Factors Affecting Option Value

Implied volatility of an option is actually not a very reliable method for predicting future movement of premium value. For anyone entering a simple buy or sell position in a put, or a more advanced spread, straddle, or ratio write, this may be troubling news. But it is a mistake to attempt to isolate the likely movement in option values based on some modeling of implied volatility. Trying to analyze options as standalone products within the market is unrealistic. In fact, many market factors affect option valuation beyond the mathematical variables involved in Black-Scholes and other option modeling formulae.

> **Key Point:** It is a mistake to try to analyze options in isolation; you have to bring a number of influences into the analysis.

At least seven factors affect option valuation beyond implied volatility. They are described in the following sections.

Stock Price Movement

The actual movement in the underlying directly affects the extrinsic value of an option and, accordingly, its overall value. This cannot be easily or simply reduced to a mathematical conclusion because the causes are intangible. Why does a stock's price behave as it does? This is the great unknown in the market. Even when specific news is known, the reaction in stock pricing is often illogical or unknown. For example, if a company misses its earnings estimates by one penny, a stock might fall by 5 percent or even 10 percent in a single day. (It is likely to recapture some or all of the price in following sessions, but the point remains that the reaction is extreme.) Most reactions to news or even rumor are going to be exaggerated and subject to later correction, but the fact remains that the basic movement in price is affected by so many intangible elements that the true "value" of a stock from day to day cannot be known.

Some academics might observe that the real value of a share of stock is the tangible book value per share, divided by the shares outstanding. This ignores the most important feature of valuation, however; that is the potential for future profits, most often summarized in the P/E ratio, or the multiple of price based on earnings per share. Value cannot be sterilized into an accounting formulation. This brings up a very important aspect to option valuation itself. If a stock's value is a combination of tangible and intangible influences including anticipation of future profits and sector strength or weakness as some of dozens of possible factors, how can an option be assigned a *reasonable* value at all? If a share of stock cannot be accurately valued in the moment, neither can an option. For this reason, the trend is much more significant than today's stock price movement. Ultimately, historical volatility is more valuable than the option's implied volatility because it provides a view of the current trend.

Stock Market Volatility and Trend

Equally important to option pricing is the overall market, its current and long-term trend in pricing, and general volatility. In recent years, markets have become more volatile than they were historically, for many reasons. They include globalization, Internet trading, expanded stock and options markets, the introduction of widespread index trading, and expanded availability of markets to a larger investing base. Consider, for example, the growth in daily volume of trading. Before market automation, it would have been impossible for exchange traders and specialists to transact a volume above a physical limit. With electronic processing and the modern dominant trend for automated order placement, there are virtually no physical limits in stock or option-based trading. This has made the stock market not only larger in terms of trading volume, but also much more volatile than in the past.

> **Key Point:** Improved speed and access to the markets have actually made them more volatile, able to handle any volume of trades, but also subject to greater uncertainty.

The Time Element

Option valuation cannot be summarized into a tidy, easily identified valuation because of the time element. This factor involves more than time value and time decay. The time element also affects changes in extrinsic value that, while also affected by the underlying volatility and overall market volatility, is going to perform differently for each class of options.

The observation that a long-term option premium is less reactive to changes in the underlying is usually associated with in-the-money options, but all options are affected by variables in time as well as by larger market trends and volatility. As expiration approaches, the uncertainties of time-based extrinsic change evaporate along with actual time value decay, but here again, this change varies with other influences. There is no easy formula that applies to every option. The desire among option traders to find a clear, concise, specific formula to understand the effects of time on premium is not possible.

The Proximity Element

No matter how much time remains to expiration, the proximity element of the option has a strong influence on premium changes as well as on implied volatility itself. This is what makes implied volatility so unreliable. Consider option price movement when the underlying is seven points out of the money versus the same option price movement when it is only one point out of the money.

The proximity of current underlying market price, to strike of the option, is one of the strongest influences on option pricing. You will observe that for most options, the proximity has more influence than most other features. This has always been the case; however, federal tax laws have made this more complex. Opening unqualified covered calls, for example, means the loss (or delay) of long-term capital gains status for the underlying, which has directly affected the trading in deep in-the-money calls and, in many strategies, deep in-the-money puts as well. Thus, a focus has emerged over several years in which emphasis in short option writing is concentrated on strikes within one increment of the current underlying price. This focus itself influences option premium values because, as with any supply and demand market, greater interest in one position over another also affects its pricing.

> **Key Point:** Proximity determines the practicality of all option strategies; this fact also changes the valuation of options due to more focus on close-to-the-money strikes.

Dividend Yield and Changes

Many option traders make the mistake of overlooking dividend yield. However, in many strategies in which profits are marginal, including those with long stock positions hedged with offsetting options, dividends may represent a large portion of overall income (sometimes more than half). The selection of one stock over another for certain strategies can be influenced by the dividend yield.

Interest Rates

Any strategy involves commitment of capital, and one method for quantifying the value of an options strategy is to compare it to rates that can be earned on other products, most often on Treasury securities. This comparison has become less important in recent years as interest rates have fallen; however, in the future, increased rates could make this more important once again.

Interest rates are an important aspect to most mathematical modeling to peg intrinsic value. Even though these are estimates to be used for comparative purposes among options and not as definitive valuation models, the role of interest rates brings the potential return from options into perspective.

Perceptions

It should not surprise anyone that perceptions of value play a major role in the actual outcome of a product, whether stock, options, debt securities, or real estate. Any product is worth whatever price a buyer and seller agree upon, and this is just as true in the options market as anywhere else. It is interesting that in the strong bear market of 2008 and 2009, when investors fled the stock market and moved assets into cash, the trading volume in options grew to record high levels. This reveals that a growing number of investors recognize the relative safety of options in comparison to stocks. The loss limitations enable you to control shares while risking far less money. In addition, options serve as an important portfolio management tool that hedges the inherent risks of stock market investing.

The perception of risk is often a self-fulfilling prophecy. The fear factor influences the market as much as any hard news on earnings, Merger and Acquisition (M&A) activity, or economic strength and weakness. Markets rely on perceptions, positive and negative, to set the tone for the current trend. The fundamentals should never be ignored in selection of stocks, whether for long-term growth or for speculation; but the fundamentals are also limited because they address the rational financial view. No value can be placed on the perception of a company, and for this reason, option valuation often benefits or suffers because the market's perception overrides the more tangible elements.

> **Key Point:** Perception has more to do with short-term price movement than any other cause. This is driven by fear, greed, and uncertainty, the primary emotions of the market.

Spotting the Overall Trend

If the purpose in using options is to hedge against risk in other positions (usually long stock), it certainly helps in your quest to gather information about price trends. If your intention is to speculate on short-term price movement, these same short-term price trends are valuable as well. The timing of spreads, straddles, and ratios (and even covered calls) determines the short-term profitability as well as overall profit or loss. In most of the strategies involving longer-term long positions serving as cover for shorter-term shorts, timing can be critical.

To effectively time your entry in to option strategies, you should bring together several important aspects of the decision into a single approach. They include

1. *Appropriate stock selection.* With options as a speculative tool, you are trading the stock rather than the company. As a tool for mitigating risk within your portfolio, options work as a management tool, protecting you against unacceptable levels of loss and, in fact, reducing the inherent market risks in volatile markets. However, in any type of market, you need to identify stocks that are a good match for your risk profile. Historical volatility is one of the best indicators for identifying market risk; this, combined with a study of some important fundamental indicators, helps pick companies as long-term value or growth investments or simply as viable candidates for option trading.

2. *Tracking of market-wide trends.* At any specific time, markets are going through periods of optimism or pessimism. Within those primary trends, contrary price runs occur as a matter of course. For example, in bear markets, you are likely to see intermediate bull trends. These false starts easily mislead investors, making timing difficult. Option traders have an advantage when picking some strategies that work in all types of markets. For example, by limiting profits, you reduce or eliminate the threat of losses as a trade-off. Given the fact that one side of an advanced strategy may be closed before the other, advanced strategies offer a two-pronged advantage in any kind of market trend. First, potential losses are limited, and second, your ability to close portions of a strategy based on price movement maximizes flexibility. Market-wide trends affect values of individual stocks, so even without giving consideration to an individual company's fundamentals, the timing of option positions based on these market trends can be profitable, while limiting exposure to risk.

3. *Awareness of a particular company and its strength or weakness within its sector.* Strong companies are likely to outperform their sectors as a whole, and by the same logic, weaker companies are going to underperform. When market-wide trends are strong in either direction, option traders can spot advantages for many hedging and speculative strategies. When you are picking a company for option strategies, the underlying and fundamental strength or weakness of that company often determines the implied volatility in options as well as market risk due to the stock's historical volatility; these important indicators show up in technical trends and patterns.

4. *Knowledge about a few important technical indicators.* Option trading often is focused on option pricing, timing, and proximity attributes, but overlooks or ignores the underlying security altogether. Many option trades are entered on a few favored companies, either residing in the portfolio or held at one time. Familiarity is not a good enough reason to pick a company's stock, however. Before you decide to trade options on one

company (whether stock is owned or not), it makes sense to study a few technical indicators for the stock and to decide whether the timing of an option strategy makes sense—or whether you should wait or select an alternative strategy.

> **Key Point:** Focusing on only a few companies for option trades is comfortable, but it also can blind you to the potential profits of a broader analysis.

Reliance on Stock-based Technical Analysis

Technical indicators—movement and patterns of price—develop in recognizable ways that anticipate the next direction. These patterns also provide indicators of strength or weakness in a developing trend. You need to be aware of only a few key technical indicators to improve the timing of your option strategies. Five of these indicators will greatly improve your ability to read price charts and to select appropriate option strategies. These indicators are support and resistance, gaps and breakouts, double tops and bottoms, head and shoulders, and volatility trends.

Support and Resistance

The trading range of a stock is defined as the space between support and resistance. *Support* is the lowest price that sellers are willing to accept, and *resistance* is the highest price that buyers are willing to pay. You can tell a lot about a stock by the breadth of its trading range. A very narrow range indicates low volatility, and a broader or growing trading range tells you the stock is far more volatile.

A trading range can evolve without changing its breadth. In other words, the breadth of trading remains the same, but the entire range trends upward or downward. For example, Colgate Palmolive (CL) saw its price levels change, but the range itself remained within a two-point breadth for most of this time. This trend is summarized in Figure 9.1.

CL- COLGATE PALMOLIVE

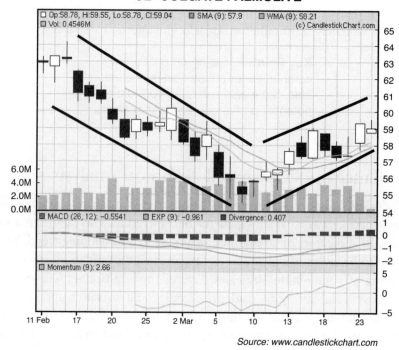

Source: www.candlestickchart.com

Figure 9.1   Narrow Trading Range, Colgate Palmolive

Even though the stock trended down and then turned and trended back up, the trading range remained about the same. Thus, neither support nor resistance changed, even though price levels were changing. The same rule can work in reverse, with a relatively wide breadth to the trading range. For example, Wal-Mart (WMT) also demonstrated a range of only a few points, as shown in Figure 9.2.

Within the broad range, price movement was quite volatile. For short-term option trading strategies, this type of short-term price volatility is very attractive. It indicates that a runaway trend is not likely, but profitable interim price changes are likely.

WMT - WAL-MART STORES

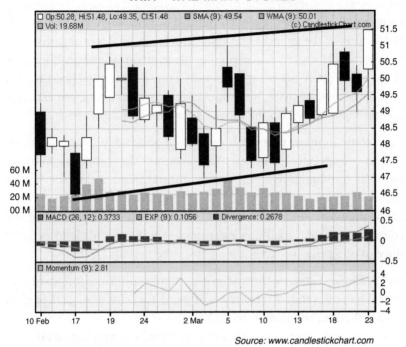

Source: www.candlestickchart.com

Figure 9.2   Wide Trading Range, Wal-Mart

Support and resistance are the defining attributes to the stock chart. They create the "normal" trading picture, and all subsequent price trends either conform to it or vary from it. The degree of change and strength of price movement are defined in terms of how they act with support and resistance. Option trades made with an awareness of support and resistance (and a stock's tendency to stay within it or move above or below it) are made more reliably.

> **Key Point:** Support and resistance are the cornerstones of technical analysis; this serves as the basis for all technical indicators.

Gaps and Breakouts

As long as price levels remain within a defined trading range, nothing exceptional occurs in the overall trend. The price direction may evolve, but as long as the support and resistance levels hold, nothing dramatic is expected. However, if a gap takes place, it can signal an important change in price. A *gap* is a space between one day's closing price and the next day's opening price. It is important because as a rule, you expect to see trading open within the range of the previous day's activity.

Gaps come in many types. A *common gap* occurs as a matter of course and has no special significance. You recognize the common gap by the fact that trading levels resume their normal trend within the trading range. A *breakaway gap* precedes a strong price movement above or below previously established levels. A *runaway gap* begins a strong and continuing trend. Finally, an *exhaustion gap* is most likely to occur at the end of a price movement away from the previous trend.

For example, Citicorp showed a gap trend within a short period of time. Figure 9.3 shows three types of gaps. Two common gaps precede a price decline, and then a strong breakaway gap follows. As prices settle into a very narrow area of trading, an exhaustion gap signals the end of the movement, followed by an upward trend.

Spotting gaps and properly identifying their meaning can provide valuable timing information for option trades in the short term, and for knowing when to take profits or cut losses when current short-term trends come to an end.

> **Key Point:** Gaps signal one- to two-day volatility and, possibly, the start of a strong change in trading patterns.

C - CITIGROUP INC

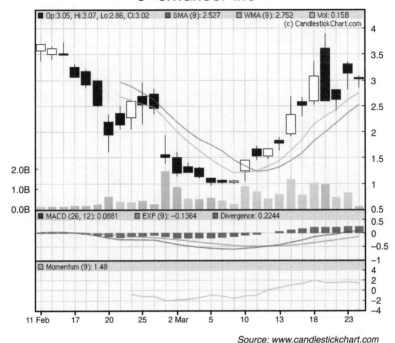

■ Op:3.05, Hi:3.07, Lo:2.86, Cl:3.02   ■ SMA (9): 2.527   □ WMA (9): 2.752   □ Vol: 0.15B
(c) CandlestickChart.com

■ MACD (26, 12): 0.0881   ■ EXP (9): –0.1364   ■ Divergence: 0.2244

□ Momentum (9): 1.48

Source: www.candlestickchart.com

Figure 9.3   Gaps, Citigroup

Double Tops and Bottoms

One of the most reliable and easiest patterns to spot in a stock chart is the *double top* or *double bottom*. The common wisdom tells traders that if price "tests" resistance twice without breaking through, it is likely to retreat and begin falling. A test means price approaches the border of the trading range without moving through it. The same argument applies on the bottom. If price tests support levels twice without breaking through, the price often precedes an uptrend.

For example, IBM's price saw a double bottom preceding a strong price run-up. This pattern is shown in Figure 9.4.

IBM - INTL BUSINESS MAC

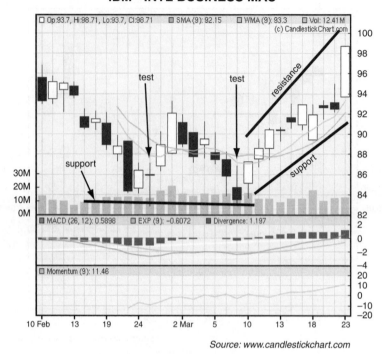

Source: www.candlestickchart.com

Figure 9.4   Double Bottom, IBM

Recognizing double tops and double bottoms helps you to time option trades to maximize profit potential or to avoid possible problems due to an emerging trend not favorable to an option-based position.

> **Key Point:** Double tests of resistance or support are important signals that prices are about to move in the opposite direction.

Head and Shoulders

Another popular chart pattern is the *head and shoulders*. This is a three-part test of resistance. The second spike (middle) actually tests the resistance line; the first and third spikes (shoulders) are below that level. If the head and shoulders occurs without breaking through resistance, it signals a likely price decline immediately afterward and move down through support.

The same is true at the support level. The reverse head and shoulders pattern consists of three downward price spikes. The middle spike (head) approaches or reaches support, and the first and third spikes (shoulders) do not fall as far. After the pattern appears, price is expected to trend in the opposite direction, upward and through the resistance level. See the Sherwin-Williams example in Figure 9.5.

Reverse Head and Shoulders

SHW - SHERWIN WILLIAMS

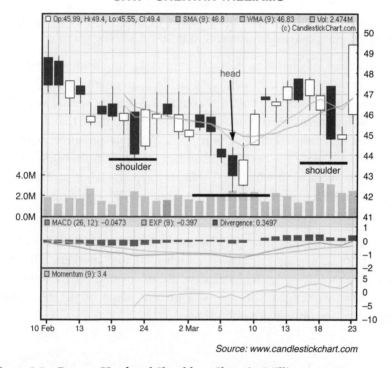

Source: www.candlestickchart.com

Figure 9.5   Reverse Head and Shoulders, Sherwin-Williams

Notice that the repeated attempts to break through support levels are followed by a strong upward trend in price. This is typical of the head and shoulders pattern. For options strategies, the head and shoulders pattern is one of the most reliable of technical indicators, and it can help improve your timing significantly.

> **Key Point:** The head and shoulders pattern is a favorite technical indicator because it is easily recognized and is a clear signal of a coming price trend.

Volatility Trends

Additional technical patterns are not as easily interpreted as the preceding ones. However, be aware of how trading ranges change. If the range begins to widen from previously established levels, this signals increasing volatility. This can spell opportunity or risk for option trading. As ranges begin to narrow, this trend indicates declining volatility.

The patterns of changing range breadth take on various shapes and sizes. They are variously described as flags, pennants, triangles, and wedges. They all refer to volatility trends and deserve special attention. Few stock patterns remain unchanged forever, and those that do tend to make rather uninteresting option plays. You rely on some degree of volatility to create the best opportunities for profit from option-based strategies. In cases in which you want to keep stock but protect paper profits, hedging strategies can be signaled by evolving volatility patterns.

The technical trends you experience can work as strong tools for timing of option strategies, especially in highly volatile markets. The next chapter examines one final strategy: the uncovered put. The various strategies involving uncovered puts present some of the best profit opportunities among all option trades.

10

UNCOVERED PUTS TO CREATE CASH FLOW: RISING MARKETS AND REVERSAL PATTERNS

A final range of strategies worth exploring is that of the short put. In chapters on spreads and straddles, short puts were shown as being covered by longer-term long puts, or even offset by short stock as a form of cover. Traders acknowledge that uncovered calls are high risk because it is impossible to know how high a stock's price can rise. The corresponding risk for uncovered puts is far lower, for four reasons:

1. *Stock prices cannot fall indefinitely.* Although uncovered call risk is in theory unlimited, uncovered put risk is less simply because there is a limit to how far a stock's price can fall. It could fall to zero if a company could be shown to be worthless.

2. *The real floor of stock prices is tangible book value per share, not zero.* As long as a company is a going concern and has tangible net worth, that creates an absolute floor for stock prices. It is quite unlikely that a stock's price will decline below this level.

3. *Lower-priced stocks contain less risk due to market risk limits.* If you limit your uncovered put writing to the lower-priced range of stocks, the dollar risk is also going to be much lower. A $150 stock with tangible book value of $25 per share has maximum risk of $125 per share; in comparison, a $15 stock with a

$3 tangible book value per share has a maximum risk of $12 per share.

4. *Time decay works for short sellers, and positions can be closed at a profit or rolled forward to avoid exercise.* Option sellers always have an advantage over buyers. Just as time works against sellers, it is the greatest benefit for sellers. The closer to expiration, the faster time decay occurs. As a result, option sellers are likely to focus on those options with two months or less to go until expiration. After time decay has occurred, a short position can be closed at a profit. In addition, a decayed-level option can be rolled forward and replaced with a later-expiring contract at the same strike or at a lower strike.

The Uncovered Short Put

The immediate response to the suggestion that writing short puts is not high risk is surprise. After all, everyone knows that writing uncovered options is a dangerous idea. Or is it?

> **Key Point:** Uncovered option writing is not always as dangerous as believed. Depending on the use of puts or calls, uncovered writes can be relatively safe, especially compared to buying long options.

Consider the case of a trader who believes stock values are going to rise. Such a trader naturally wants to be positioned long in the market, but if that trader's portfolio is also depressed, buying more shares is a troubling idea. In addition, it may be the case that all this trader's capital is tied up in shares of stock currently valued below original basis. If you limit your trading to stocks only, you would have to pass on the opportunity in this situation. However, using uncovered puts, you can still take part in an upward-trending market.

You can take part by buying calls, a relatively easy and very basic strategy. However, buying calls also requires capital, even though it is much less than the equivalent purchase of stock. Another method for exploiting rising markets is to sell uncovered puts. The margin requirements for this are covered by existing stock positions, which may be the best use for depreciated shares. You need to wait out a rise in market values before you will be able to get back to your basis, so you have to accept dividends and simply hope for an improvement in your portfolio valuation. This may take months and in some cases, even years.

When you sell an uncovered put, you give the buyer on the other side of the transaction the right to sell 100 shares to you at the fixed strike, even if the market value has fallen far below that strike. This "buyer" is actually the Options Clearing Corporation (OCC), which acts as the clearinghouse for all options trading. It acts as buyer to every seller and as seller to every buyer. When someone who owns a put exercises it, the OCC assigns the put to a short seller. The OCC automatically exercises in-the-money puts on the day of exercise. So if your short put ends up in the money, it will get exercised.

> **Key Point:** If your short option ends up in the money, it will be exercised before it expires. Even if there is only a small number of long option holders, the OCC steps in and exercises all in-the-money positions.

This does not mean exercise is always automatic; you can close the position or roll it forward to avoid exercise. Viewed as a standalone trade, a short put is not difficult to manage. Given the ever-present risk of early exercise, a prudent approach to exercise avoidance is to close or roll a put as it approaches the money, instead of waiting until it has already gone in the money. Your maximum exposure level is equal to the strike, minus the premium you received when you opened the uncovered position. Because you receive the premium, you can accept exercise down to the breakeven limit (without considering trading costs). For example, if you sell a 20 put for 2, your breakeven point is 18 (and your loss risk begins below 18):

Strike of the put	20
Less: credit received	−2
Breakeven price	18

The uncovered put is similar to the uncovered call in the sense that (a) you receive the credit, (b) your belief in price movement of the stock makes the strategy viable, and (c) you accept a degree of risk in opening the position. The best chances for profit are going to be found when you open an uncovered put out of the money. Here, you face the same dilemma that any short trader has to manage: If you go far out of the money, risk is greatly reduced. But the further out you go, the lower the premium. The most favorable range of prices occurs when the put is less than five points out of the money. The expiration is equally important; you want rapid time decay, meaning your greatest advantage is found in puts expiring in three months or less.

Balancing the issues of proximity and time as an offset to cost (in this case, the "cost" is actually your benefit because you receive the payment) is a constant problem in trading options. Obviously, getting a large return for writing in-the-money uncovered puts is attractive initially, but it carries the burden of likely exercise, perhaps even early exercise as a reality. The only time it makes sense to write uncovered in-the-money puts is when nonintrinsic value (the combination of time and extrinsic value) is exceptionally high and you expect an adjustment to take place quickly, making it possible to profit from selling the put now. Even so, exposing yourself to exercise at a price above market value (when exercise will take place) is justified only if and when you are also willing to purchase shares at the strike.

> **Key Point:** A basic theme to any short put writing is that you must be willing to acquire 100 shares at the strike; otherwise, uncovered short puts do not make sense.

This raises an equally important issue when you sell uncovered puts: You should limit this activity to stocks of companies you would like to acquire. Option trading focuses on the stock and not on the company, as a general rule. But when you sell uncovered puts, you are exposing yourself to the risk of having shares put to you at the strike. Because of this, the company should be one you would be happy to acquire, based on fundamentals and long-term value and growth potential. You limit the range of companies for short put writing by comparing a short list of fundamentals, including revenue and net profit trend, working capital tests (current ratio or quick assets ratio), debt ratio, P/E ratio, and dividend yield. These trends alone enable you to reduce a list of potential stocks for uncovered put writing down to a small handful. If you require constant growth in operating statement trends as well as consistency in working capital and long-term debt trends, a P/E below 20, and dividend yield above 3 percent (for example), you will end up with fewer than 10 to 20 stocks to choose from. These fundamentals isolate the strongest, best-managed companies with the best potential for strong market performance, which becomes important if your short puts are exercised.

Evaluating Your Rate of Return from Selling Puts

Your net return from writing uncovered calls varies with the holding period. Some traders believe that longer holding periods yield better returns, but in fact the opposite is true. Longer holding periods yield more cash due to higher time value; but returns tend to be higher for shorter-term uncovered calls, especially those nearest to the money.

For example, Wal-Mart (WMT) was valued at $52 per share when the following puts were available:

Two-month 50 put	1.82
Three-month 50 put	2.47
Six-month 50 put	4.25

The 50 strike is the most desirable at this point; these are two points out of the money, which is the ideal proximity for writing uncovered puts. However, which yields the best return? The 4.25 put is the highest amount of cash, but it is not the best yield. To make a valid and accurate comparison, calculate *annualized* yields. This calculation requires that the yield be divided by the holding period in months and then multiplied by 12 (months). This restates the yield as though all comparisons were held for one full year. Applying this to the example of Wal-Mart 50 puts:

$$\text{Two-month 50 put} \quad 1.82 \left((1.82 \div 50) \div 2 \right) \times 12 = 21.8\%$$
$$\text{Three-month 50 put} \quad 2.47 \left((2.47 \div 50) \div 3 \right) \times 12 = 19.8\%$$
$$\text{Six-month 50 put} \quad 4.25 \left((4.25 \div 50) \div 6 \right) \times 12 = 17.0\%$$

This result is typical. The shorter-term near-the-money puts yield higher net returns than those further out. In all cases, the entire premium is nonintrinsic (consisting of a mix of time and extrinsic value). However, the two-month premium will decay at a much greater rate than either the three-month or the six-month examples. Because of this, you get the best yield, *and* you have the shortest risk exposure of any of the other choices. In fact, leaving an uncovered position open for as long as six months is problematic for several reasons. There is the chance the stock's value will decline, requiring you to take a loss or roll forward to avoid exercise. The longer term also ties up your risk capital for a longer term. Finally, the margin requirement ties up other capital in your portfolio for as long as the position remains open. You maximize the uncovered short put by writing a two-month strike at the closest out-of-the-money position.

Reviewing another stock, you quickly realize that the benefits of shorter-term short puts are apparent. In the case of IBM, whose market value was $98.78, the 95 puts yielded the following returns:

Two-month 95 put $\quad 4.10 \left((4.10 \div 95) \div 2 \right) \times 12 = 25.9\%$
Four-month 95 put $\quad 6.80 \left((6.80 \div 95) \div 4 \right) \times 12 = 21.5\%$
Seven-month 95 put $\quad 9.30 \left((9.30 \div 95) \div 7 \right) \times 12 = 16.8\%$

Even with higher stock prices and richer dollar-value options, the net outcome remains the same. Shorter-term short puts yield better than longer-term ones. The yield in each of these cases is expressed based on the strike; that will be the exercise price if the stock price declines. For later calculations, the yield based on strike (exercised basis) added to the dividend yield produces the true overall yield on the exercised position.

The dollar value of very long-term puts is quite high, but once again, the long-term yield fades in comparison to very short-term yield. The SPDR Gold Shares (GLD) share price was $91.30 when the following 90 puts could be sold:

Two-month 90 put	4.09	$((4.09 \div 90) \div 2) \times 12 = 27.3\%$
Three-month 90 put	5.70	$((5.70 \div 90) \div 3) \times 12 = 25.3\%$
Six-month 90 put	8.56	$((8.56 \div 90) \div 6) \times 12 = 19.0\%$
Nine-month 90 put	11.10	$((11.10 \div 90) \div 9) \times 12 = 16.4\%$
Ten-month 90 put	11.70	$((11.70 \div 90) \div 10) \times 12 = 15.6\%$
Twenty-two-month 90 put	17.20	$((17.20 \div 90) \div 22) \times 12 = 10.4\%$

This example demonstrates that even when stock prices are approximately the same between two issues (IBM compared to GLD), the returns are still better with short-term uncovered puts. In fact, when the annualized comparison is extended out to LEAPS puts, the returns continue to diminish over time. When you consider the burden of leaving a short put position open as long as 22 months, for a net yield under 40 percent of the return from the two-month put, the shorter exposure makes sense.

> **Key Point:** The high returns on an annualized basis should not be assumed to represent your typical and expected return. This exercise is valuable for comparison purposes, not as a guaranteed rate of return from short put writing.

This also allows you to write a series of subsequent short puts based on evolving price levels. As long as the gap between current price and strike remains, these are out of the money and safe from exercise. The risk of loss occurs only after the put moves in the money and absorbs the premium. In the case of GLD, for example, the breakeven is the strike minus the credit for selling the put:

Strike of the short put	90.00
Less: premium received	−4.09
Breakeven price	85.91

Breakeven on the two-month put uncovered write is 5.39 points below the level at the time the puts were reviewed. This gives you a lot of point spread to close the position or to roll it forward, and you only have to wait out two months until expiration, a period when time value will evaporate very rapidly.

Covered Short Straddles

The uncovered put can be designed with flexibility and minimum risk, especially compared to an uncovered call. One strategy offering great flexibility is the covered short straddle. This title is inaccurate in the sense that it is not completely covered; in fact, the put is uncovered but matched up with a short call that is covered.

> **Key Point:** A "covered" short straddle consists of a covered call and an *uncovered* short put. The position cannot be completely covered.

The covered short straddle consists of three parts: 100 shares of the underlying stock, a short call, and a short put. The strike should be as close as possible to the current price of the stock; one or the other of the short positions will always be in the money, but maximum profit will be earned due to a decline in time value in both short options. The closer to the money each position remains, the safer the position. This requires, of course, that the underlying stock price will not move too much in either direction.

For example, Best Buy (BBY) was priced at $37.96 per share when the following two-month options were available:

37.50 call	3.30
37.50 put	2.95
Total	6.25

This is a very impressive return based on the 37.50 strike: 16.7 percent in only two months or over 100 percent annualized. This comparison is useful only for evaluating a strategy between two or more stocks. The assumption that an option strategy will yield a 100 percent return would be reckless because (a) you cannot necessarily duplicate this two-month return six times in one year; (b) exercise of any short position changes the whole picture; and (c) subsequent action (closing a position, rolling it forward, or accepting exercise) will also change final outcomes.

Key Point: Any short position's outcome is going to be affected by closing one or more of the options, early exercise, conversion to another strategy, or rolling forward.

If you enter a covered straddle, buying 100 shares and selling both options, your net cost is

100 shares	$3,796
Less: 37.50 call	− 330
Less: 37.50 put	− 295
Total	$3,171

The covered straddle is a relatively safe position. The call is covered, so there is no upside risk (although upside profit is capped by the short call). The downside risk does not begin until you have moved through the net basis, which is $3,796 minus the credit for the two options: 3,796 − 625 = 3,171. Normally, a covered call would be written above your net basis in stock; in this example, it is 46 cents below, assuming you buy 100 shares at the current price. If you had purchased shares of Best Buy previously, potential profits from the covered straddle would be far greater. Table 10.1 summarizes the profit and loss zones for this position.

Table 10.1   Best Buy ($37.96 per share)—Covered Short Straddle

Price	Short Option Positions 37.50 Call	Short Option Positions 37.50 Put	Net
$45	$0	$295	$295
44	0	295	295
43	0	295	295
42	0	295	295
41	0	295	295
40	80	295	375
39	180	295	475
38	280	295	575

Table 10.1   Continued

| | Short Option Positions | | |
Price	37.50 Call	37.50 Put	Net
37	330	245	575
36	330	145	475
35	330	45	375
34	330	−55	275
33	330	−155	175
32	330	−255	75
31	330	−355	−25
30	330	−455	−125
29	330	−555	−225
28	330	−655	−325

The higher-price losses in the call were capped at zero because exercise is covered by the 100 shares of stock. The overall profit and loss is based on the strikes of 37.50 and not on the actual basis in the stock. Considering the wide profit margin, extending from $32 per share upward, makes the short straddle attractive. The upside profit is capped at the credit for the short put. However, in the event of exercise at $37.50, you retain the full credit for both short positions, $625. The downside risk is managed without trouble because the short put can be closed after time value evaporates, rolled forward, or left alone and allowed to exercise. The exercise alternative would result in your buying 100 shares at $37.50 per share, at a time when market value was below that level.

> **Key Point:** A key to avoiding loss in a covered short straddle is to close positions after time value has fallen and, if necessary, to avoid exercise by rolling or closing the short early. Remember, one of the sides is always in the money.

Rolling this position forward extends one or both strikes. If the stock price rises, the short call can be replaced with a later-expiring 37.50 or 40 strike. If the stock price falls, the put can be replaced with a later-expiring 37.50 or 35 strike. Rolling either position converts the straddle into a vertical or diagonal spread, and closing either position converts it into a simple covered call or uncovered put. Extending expiration by rolling forward gives you the advantage of avoiding exercise or extending the strike to a more profitable level if and when exercise does occur. It has the disadvantage of extending the time the position remains open.

Another adjustment to the strategy would be to close one of the short positions at a profit when time value has evaporated (most likely the out-of-the-money side) and then open another, later-expiring position with more time value. In this manner, you can perpetually roll one side to subsequent two- or three-month short positions, while also rolling out of the in-the-money short side (or later closing at a profit due to declined time value).

An uncovered straddle write involves short call and put positions without the benefit of owning 100 shares of stock. This greatly increases risk because, like the covered straddle, one of the two short options is always going to be in the money. Thus, early exercise is always a possibility. In addition, the uncovered position exposes you to the possibility of a runaway price movement in either direction. With the covered straddle, you have upside protection with coverage of the call. In the uncovered position, price movement occurring in either direction poses a threat. Although the uncovered position looks attractive on paper, it is conceivably a far greater risk simply because the call is uncovered.

Covered Short Spreads

An adjustment to the short put strategy is the covered short spread. While the covered short straddle employs identical strikes, the covered short spread can be easily built with both call and put out of the money. This creates the desirable situation in which a premium consisting entirely of time value can be expected to decline sharply (especially if you limit this strategy to two- or three-month expirations). The profit zone is far greater in this strategy; it is conceivable that both short positions can remain out of the money all the way to expiration.

> **Key Point:** Covered short spreads have wider profit zones than straddles because of the gap between short strikes. This makes the short spread lower risk and enables you to avoid exercise more effectively.

Exercise will not occur as long as both sides are out of the money. This is obvious, of course, but it is worth mentioning because a secondary strategy may be employed to ensure that exercise doesn't become possible while the positions remain open and once stock prices begin to move toward one of the strikes. To avoid exercise, one or both positions can be closed at a profit after the current price of the underlying approaches or reaches the strike. Second, the short position can also be closed and rolled forward. Considering the broader expanse of profit zone for the short spread, a vertical roll makes sense as time value is going to fall out of the position. The only time to go diagonal (up an increment for a short call or down for a short put) is if the stock appears to be trending further in the current direction.

An example of the covered short spread: Burlington Northern Santa Fe (BNI) was priced at $60.74 and the following two-month options were available:

65 call	2.75
55 put	2.35
Total	5.10

The covered short spread also assumes that you own 100 shares of the underlying. The short positions discount your basis by 5.10 points. With the position expiring in two months, that is a net return (based on an average of the strikes of $60 per share) of 8.5 percent, or annualized 51.0 percent. Table 10.2 summarizes the profit and loss zones for this position:

Table 10.2 Burlington Northern Santa Fe ($60.74 per share)—Covered Short Spread

| | Short Option Positions | | |
Price	Three 65 Call	Two 55 Put	Net
$70	$0	$235	$235
69	0	235	235
68	0	235	235
67	75	235	310
66	175	235	410
65	275	235	510
64	275	235	510
63	275	235	510
62	275	235	510
61	275	235	510
60	275	235	510
59	275	235	510
58	275	235	510
57	275	235	510
56	275	235	510
55	275	235	510
54	275	135	410
53	275	35	310
52	275	−65	210
51	275	−165	110
50	275	−265	10
49	275	−365	−90

Table 10.2 Continued

	Short Option Positions		
	Three	Two	
Price	65 Call	55 Put	Net
48	275	−465	−190
47	275	−565	−290

The short spread has many characteristics similar to the short straddle. The upside profit is limited due to the fact that the short call is covered. The downside risk does not kick in until the stock's price has fallen to $49 per share, more than 11 points below value at the time the position was first reviewed. As with the straddle, either short option can be closed after time value has fallen, allowed to exercise, or rolled forward to avoid exercise. However, no action is required as long as the stock's price remains between the 10-point range from $55 to $65 per share. At this range, the full credit for the two short options is in place, and both options remain out of the money.

> **Key Point:** As long as the stock's market value remains between the short option strikes, the position is safe. As price approaches one of the strikes, it makes sense to close the short position or roll it forward.

Rolling forward vertically extends both time value and expiration; rolling a call up one increment or rolling a put down one increment converts the position to a diagonal short spread. Closing one side or the other undoes the spread and creates a covered call or ownership of 100 shares and an uncovered put.

Although creating a ratio write for the previously described short straddle introduces significant risk (because one side or the other is always in the money), a ratio write for the short spread is quite profitable and contains less risk, notably if the ratio occurs on the covered call side. For example, if you own 200 shares of the underlying, the 3-to-2 ratio would consist of three short calls and two short puts. Total credit for this is

Three 65 calls	8.25		
Two 55 puts	4.70		
Total	12.95		

Table 10.3 summarizes the outcome of the ratio short covered spread.

Table 10.3   Burlington Northern Santa Fe, 200 shares ($60.74 per share)—Ratio Covered Short Spread

	Short Option Positions		
Price	Three 65 Call	Two 55 Put	Net
$69	$–700	$470	$–230
69	–600	470	–130
69	–500	470	–30
69	–400	470	70
69	–300	470	170
70	–200	470	270
69	–100	470	370
68	–75	470	395
67	225	470	695
66	525	470	995
65	825	470	1,295
64	825	470	1,295
63	825	470	1,295
62	825	470	1,295
61	825	470	1,295
60	825	470	1,295
59	825	470	1,295
58	825	470	1,295
57	825	470	1,295

Table 10.3   Continued

	Short Option Positions		
Price	Three 65 Call	Two 55 Put	Net
56	825	470	1,295
55	825	470	1,295
54	825	270	1,095
53	825	70	895
52	825	−130	695
51	825	−330	495
50	825	−530	295
49	825	−730	95
48	825	−930	−105
47	825	−1,130	−305
46	825	−1,330	−505
45	825	−1,530	−705

The ratio version of this strategy gives you a 20-point profit range in the example. However, unlike the limit on upside risk, the ratio creates a risk equal to one uncovered call (three short calls were written against 200 shares of stock). Even so, the very wide range of profitable outcomes makes this ratio much less risky than an uncovered ratio or a ratio on the put side (in which all short put positions would be uncovered). Because all options in this example are out of the money and extend only two months, decline in time value will be quite rapid.

> **Key Point:** A short ratio is less risky in the covered short spread than in a covered call because the added premium from writing both calls and puts extends the profit zone.

A number of possible outcomes include

- Covering the uncovered call or closing it at a profit to equalize the positions
- Closing either short calls or short puts if underlying price begins to approach either strike
- Waiting out expiration and taking on action
- Rolling either side forward to avoid exercise if the underlying price approaches either strike

The very large profit zone makes this strategy an insulated one. The high credit of $1,295 remains in effect for the full 10-point range between the two strikes. Even traders who are normally shy about covered call ratio writes will recognize the important differences in the short spread. The additional premium and wide range between the two strikes makes this a relatively safe strategy. If neither side ends up being exercised (meaning underlying price remains between $55 and $65 per share for the next two months), total return (based on average strike of 60 and not counting dividend yield which, in the BNI example, was approximately 2.7 percent) will be 21.6 percent, which annualizes out to 129.6 percent. As with all cases of annualizing option profitability, it is valuable as a way to compare strategies to one another or between different stocks. But it should not be assumed to serve as a consistent rate of return overall. Early exercise, closing of short positions, or modification through rolling, all alter the profit that you will realize if the position is left intact through expiration.

Recovery Strategies for Exercised Covered Straddles and Spreads

Whether you write short straddles or spreads, it is entirely possible to realize a net loss. Even if upside risk is completely hedged with a covered call position, downside risk remains a reality. For example, a stock's price may fall below breakeven and the short put exercised. In this case, you end up being required to buy shares of stock at a price above current market value.

> **Key Point:** You avoid net losses by closing or rolling options; however, if you do lose on a short straddle or spread, you can recover your paper loss with subsequent option-based strategies.

Recovery strategies are based on the assumption that you take no action to avoid exercise. The most likely among these are closing the short as the stock's price begins to decline to eliminate the risk, or to roll the short put forward (and possibly, down one increment). Rolling forward does extend the period of exposure, but it avoids having the short put exercised. Waiting out the decline may prove to be profitable if and when the stock's price rebounds or, even without a complete rebound, waiting for time value to fall enough to make a small profit or break even.

In some instances, however, these steps are not taken and you end up having stock put to you above current market value. A recovery strategy may be passive, simply holding on to shares in the hope that prices will recover, or a strategy can be much more aggressive. For example, if you had written a covered straddle or spread based on ownership of 100 shares and the short put was exercised, you end up with 200 shares. Here is a point to keep in mind:

> *Your net cost is not the exercise price.* The true net basis in your 200 shares of stock consists of the cost of the original 100 shares, plus the cost of stock put to you, minus the premium you received for selling the short position. Returning to the example of the Burlington Northern covered short spread, your basis in the first 100 shares was $6,074 (assuming you bought shares at the same time the position was opened). Your profit from the spread was $510, and an exercised put would have a basis of $5,500. Your 200 shares have a net basis of
>
> $$(\$6,074 + \$5,500 - \$ 510) \div 2 \ (200 \text{ shares}) = \$5,532$$
>
> Even if the current value of stock was as low as $50 per share, opening a subsequent covered short spread (based on strikes of 60 for the call and 50 for the put) will more than offset this net position at about five points above market value. Using the equivalent values as the previous example (which generated $510 in premium), a similar position using 200 shares could be expected to generate approximately $1,000 in premium. This offsets the loss in market value when the short put was exercised in the original covered short spread.

> **Key Point:** Recovery strategies are not as
> practical as simply avoiding exercise to
> begin with. When you close short positions
> approaching the money or roll forward,
> exercise becomes a remote possibility
> rather than a sure thing.

A danger in this recovery strategy is that it merely returns you to your original position. You have 200 shares with a net average basis of $55.32 per share, and you have now opened a new covered short spread. Your best-case outcome will be expiration of both short options. Even with this outcome, however, you have made no profit on the position. Your net basis is merely reduced to approximately the market value at the time of the second covered short spread:

$$((\$5,532 \times 2 \ (200 \ \text{shares})) - \$1,000) \div 2 \ (200 \ \text{shares}) = \$5,032$$

The limited risk of either covered straddle or spread makes these positions attractive. They both offer the potential for profit. However, accepting a loss and then attempting to recover it through an expanded short strategy is of questionable value. Recovery is possible through subsequent positions, but it would be far more practical to avoid the loss in the initial strategy by following a few prudent steps:

1. Watch the movement in the stock's price. If it approaches either strike, take action right away; don't wait hoping price will retreat.

2. Be aware that early exercise is always possible after the underlying price moves above the call's strike or below the put's strike.

3. Sell the short position when the underlying price approaches the strike, taking a small profit from decline in time value rather than risking exercise.

4. Roll forward to defer exercise. Consider rolling a call's strike up or a put's strike down to further avoid a potential loss on either side.

These steps make much more sense than waiting out the position and allowing a net loss to occur. Given the wide range of the profit zone, most situations enable you to avoid losses by taking action at the right time, *before* any of the short options end up in the money.

Short Puts in Rising Markets: One-Sided Swing Trading

Many possible applications for short puts allow you to expand your portfolio management capabilities. Whether you hedge losses with insurance puts, create low-risk strategies with covered short put positions, or employ a straddle or spread, the many uses of puts expand either long-term investment value or short-term speculation. Most important of all, puts (and calls) can be used to help avoid large losses in volatile markets.

> **Key Point:** The many flexible put-based strategies are valuable as devices for managing in highly volatile markets. It is likely in the future that markets will be more volatile than in the past, making option strategies more valuable than ever.

Short puts, for example, are very strong devices for hedging a bull market but without needing to buy shares of stock. Timing is always a problem, and many investors want to own shares but are fearful of either a sudden and unexpected long-term bear market (as it occurred beginning in 2008, for example) or even a bear intermediate trend within a bull market. Either of these situations can and does occur, and if you limit your portfolio to long holdings of stock, you are vulnerable to sharp price declines.

Puts further improve the profitability of swing trading while vastly reducing the risk of shorting stock. Because options cost much less than 100 shares of stock, options leverage a swing trading strategy. This demonstrates the point that speculation does not always have to be high risk. On the contrary, puts can mitigate or entirely remove risk. For example, the old-style shorting of stock has always been just as risky as selling uncovered calls. In addition, because it is a cumbersome transaction requiring you to borrow shares from your broker and pay interest, shorting stock is not necessary in the modern day availability of puts. With high-speed Internet and instantaneous order placement and price tracking, option trading has become affordable and practical for most investors. If you have previously avoided options because of perceived high risks, you may want to look at this situation anew and reconsider.

The put is an incredibly flexible instrument that, much like the call, can be applied in a wide range of different strategies. Short put risk is lower than short call risk, and spread or straddle strategies provide potentially high returns, especially in covered positions (remembering, of course, that a "covered" straddle or spread is really a combination of a covered call and an uncovered put). Impressive double-digit returns are not only possible, but quite safe. Such advanced strategies demand experience and market knowledge, but increasingly, the use of options is changing the face of the market.

For example, in 2008 and 2009, while stock prices were plummeting, option trading volume increased at record levels. Daily volume at the CBOE for all options traded was 2,707,491 in 2006. This increased by over one million per day in 2007, to daily average volume of 3,771,849. And in 2008, when stocks were pounded in one of the worst bear markets in decades, the CBOE option trading volume increased to an average of 4,736,703 contracts per day.[1]

> **Key Point:** At the height of the 2008 and 2009 bear market, trillions of dollars were taken out of stocks and kept on the sidelines. At the same time, volume in option trading was growing at record rates.

The strong expansion of option trading, including both calls and puts, demonstrates the widespread and practical use of options to augment returns from a stock-based portfolio. Options provide a range of valuable functions, including risk hedges and speculative strategies that range widely among degrees of risk. Even with an emphasis among many investors on call-based strategies, you should not ignore the importance and value of puts. In combination, options make the case that it is possible to create and generate profits in any type of market and as a part of any type of trend. Volatility is troubling to long-term stock investors, but to option traders, volatility only points the way to more strategies and the generation of more profits.

---

[1] Source: Chicago Board Options Exchange, at www.cboe.com, historical data (daily total volume).

GLOSSARY

annualized basis   A calculated rate of return based on a holding period of one full year; the rate is divided by the holding period (in months) and then multiplied by 12.

antistraddle rules   Tax regulations that affect the long-term favorable tax treatment of stock when an unqualified in-the-money covered call is written before the long-term period has been reached.

assignment   Exercise against a seller's short position, performed on the basis of procedures developed by the Options Clearing Corporation and brokerage firms.

at the money   An option whose strike is identical to the underlying stock's value.

automatic exercise   A form of exercise on the day of expiration, in which the Options Clearing Corporation initiates exercise of in-the-money options.

bear spread   A strategy involving the purchase and sale of options, made up of calls or puts. The position is expected to become profitable when the value of the underlying stock declines.

beta   A measure of a stock's relative volatility, comparing price movement to a larger index of market price movements.

book value   The value of a company, capital (assets less liabilities), divided by the number of outstanding shares of stock.

box spread   A position combining a bull spread and a bear spread, opened simultaneously on the same underlying stock.

breakeven price The price of stock when option positions are open. For call trades, it is the points above strike equal to call premium; for put trades, it is the points below strike price equal to the put premium.

breakout The movement of price below support or above resistance.

bull spread A strategy consisting of purchase and sale of calls or puts. It is expected to become profitable when the underlying stock rises.

butterfly spread A strategy consisting of option positions in three strikes. The strategy normally reduces or eliminates losses while maximizing profits.

buyer Anyone with a long position in stock or options; profits are derived from upward movement in stock or calls, or from downward movement in puts.

calendar spread A time spread, consisting of the simultaneous opening of long or short option positions with different expirations.

call An option allowing but not requiring a buyer to purchase 100 shares of a specified underlying stock at a fixed price and before a specific expiration date.

called away Assignment of stock through exercise of a call. At exercise, call sellers are required to deliver 100 shares of stock at the strike price.

capital gains Investment profits, taxed the same as other income if the holding period is less than one year, or at lower rates if investments were owned for one year or more.

capped-style option Any option on which exercise is allowed only during a brief period of time; if the option's value reaches cap level before expiration, exercise is automatic.

carry-over capital losses Those capital losses in excess of $3,000 net per year, carried over and applied to profits in future tax years.

chartist A technical analyst who uses price charts to anticipate upcoming price changes and directions for a stock.

class All the options traded on an underlying stock.

closing purchase transaction A transaction to buy a position and close a short position.

closing sale transaction A transaction to close a long position.

collar   A spread consisting of long stock, a covered short call, and a long put. A collar limits both maximum gains and losses.

combination   The purchase or sale of options with nonidentical terms.

condor spread   A type of butterfly spread with different strikes in short positions on both sides of a long middle strike.

contract   An option, the agreement specifying the terms for both buyer and seller. These terms include naming the underlying stock, premium cost, expiration date, and fixed strike.

conversion   Moving assigned stock from the seller of a call or to the seller of a put.

cover   Status of a short call when the trader also owns 100 shares of the underlying stock, or when a long position of the same or later expiration is open as well.

covered call   A short call when the seller also owns 100 shares of stock or holds corresponding long positions at the same or a later expiration, and at the same or a higher strike.

credit spread   A spread when net receipts from short positions are greater than premiums paid for long positions.

current market value   The day's market value of stock.

cycle   The monthly pattern of option expiration dates, consisting of the next two months and then quarterly. There are three four-month interval cycles: (1) January, April, July, and October, or JAJO; (2) February, May, August, and November, or FMAN; and (3) March, June, September, and December, or MJSD. In addition, LEAPS options always expire in January of the following two years.

debit spread   A spread for which receipts from short positions are lower than premiums paid for long positions.

deep in the money   Option status when the underlying stock's market value is more than one strike increment above a call's strike or below a put's strike.

deep out   Option status when the underlying stock's market value is more than one strike increment below a call's strike or above a put's strike.

delivery   Change in ownership of stock due to purchase, sale, or exercise of an option.

delta   The level of change in option value compared to change in the underlying stock. If the option's price change exceeds the underlying, it is an "up delta" for calls or a "down delta" for puts.

diagonal spread   Any calendar spread with long and short positions, both having different strikes and expiration dates.

discount   A reduction in the net basis of stock, caused by selling an option. This reduces the breakeven point and risk exposure for short selling of options.

dividend yield   Dividends paid; to compute, divide dividends per share by the current value per share of stock. Because dividends often represent a major portion of overall yield from option positions on long stock, this should be included in comparisons between stocks for similar strategies.

downside protection   A form of protection of long stock achieved by buying insurance puts. For every point the stock falls, intrinsic value of the put increases by one point. The put can be sold to offset stock losses, or exercised with stock sold at the strike.

early exercise   A form of exercise of an option before expiration date.

exercise   Buying stock under the terms of a call or selling stock under the terms of a put option, both occurring at a fixed strike price.

expiration date   The date when options becomes worthless.

extrinsic value   The portion of an option's premium excluding both intrinsic value and time value; volatility value of the option.

hedge   Any strategy opening one position to protect another by offsetting loss with gain. Popular hedges include buying puts to protect long stock, or using spreads and straddles to limit potential losses in stock.

horizontal spread   A calendar spread with long and short positions with the same strikes but different expiration dates.

in the money   Status of a call when the underlying stock's value is higher than the strike, or of a put when the underlying stock's value is lower than the strike.

intrinsic value   The part of an option's value equal to the number of points in the money.

last trading day   The Friday before the third Saturday of the expiration month.

LEAPS   Long-term Equity Anticipation Securities; long-term options with expiration up to 30 months.

leverage   The use of capital in a way employing a limited amount of money to control larger positions. This consists of borrowing or opening options, which each controls 100 shares of stock.

listed option   Any option traded on a public exchange.

long hedge   Purchase of options to insure a long stock position from price decline (with a long put) or to insure a short position from price rise (with a long call).

long position   Ownership of stock or options. The long position is closed by later entering a sell order, or in the case of options by exercise or expiration.

long straddle   Buying an identical number of calls and puts with the same strike and expiration, which is expected to become profitable when the underlying stock moves in either direction.

long-term capital gains   Profits on investments held for 12 months or more.

loss zone   The price range of an option when the stock price moves in an undesired direction.

margin   A brokerage account providing collateral for leveraged positions in stocks and options.

market order   An order to buy or sell at the best available price.

married put   A put hedging a long stock position.

money spread   A vertical spread.

naked option   A short call when the seller does not own 100 shares of the underlying stock, or a short put when the seller is not also short on 100 shares of the stock.

offsetting positions   Straddles subject to restrictions of deductibility of tax losses. Such losses have to be deferred until the opposite side of the transaction has been closed, to prevent traders from setting up losses in one year and profits in the following year.

open interest   The number of open option contracts used as an indicator of market interest.

open position   A trade that has not been closed, exercised, or allowed to expire.

opening purchase transaction   Any transaction to buy stock or options.

opening sale transaction   Any initial transaction to short stock or options.

option   A contract to buy (call) or to sell (put) 100 shares of stock at a specified, fixed price and by a specified date in the future. Each option refers to a specific underlying stock.

out of the money   A call when the underlying stock's value is lower than the strike, or a put when the underlying stock's value is higher than the strike.

paper profits   Any profits based on changes between opening of a position and current value, but that have not been realized by closing those positions.

premium   The option's current price. The premium is the dollar value per share, stated without dollar signs; thus, when an option is at "3," it means its current market value is $3 per share; because options refer to 100 shares, "3" is equal to $300.

price/earnings ratio (P/E)   Indicator of stock value and risk. To calculate, divide the current market value per share by the most recent earnings per share; P/E is expressed as a single numerical value. For example, current price per share is $55.14 and the EPS is $3.14. P/E is 17.6: (55.14 ÷ 3.13 = 17.6). This is the "multiple" of earnings. Current value is at a multiple of 17.6 times earnings.

profit zone   The price range of an option when the underlying stock price has moved in a desired direction.

put   An option granting the buyer the right but not the obligation to sell 100 shares of a specified underlying stock at a fixed strike price and before a specific expiration date.

put to seller   The action of exercise of a put; the seller is required to buy 100 shares of stock at the fixed strike price.

qualified covered call   In tax law, a covered call that allows long-term gain rates upon sale of stock or that allows the period counting up to a long-term holding period to continue to run. Qualification is set by time to expiration and by the price difference between market value of the stock and strike of the call. Deep in-the-money calls are unqualified.

rate of return   Yield, calculated by dividing profit upon sale by the basis of stock, options, or combinations of both.

ratio calendar combination spread   A strategy containing a ratio between long and short options, and a box spread. Long and short option positions are opened with a different number of contracts and with two or more different expiration dates.

ratio calendar spread   A strategy consisting of a varying number of options between long and short, and with different expiration dates. This creates separate profit and loss zone ranges for each expiration.

ratio write   An option strategy with partial rather than full coverage. Overall risk is reduced, but the strategy consists of covered and uncovered positions opened together.

realized profits   Those profits taken by closing a position.

resistance   A stock's highest trading price within the current trading range.

return if exercised   The rate of return from covered calls in the event a call is exercised. This includes capital gain or loss from sale of stock, dividends, and premium from selling the call.

return if unchanged   The rate of return call sellers earn if not exercised. The calculation includes dividends earned on underlying stock and the premium received for selling the call.

reverse hedge   An extended long or short hedge when more options are opened than the number needed to cover stock; this increases profit in the event of unfavorable movement in the underlying stock's price.

risk tolerance   The level and type of risk a trader is able to afford.

roll down   The replacement of a short put with another with a lower strike.

roll forward   The replacement of a short call or put with another with the same strike, but a later expiration.

roll up   The replacement of a short call with another with a higher strike.

seller A trader granting rights under an option contract; the seller profits if the value of the stock moves below the strike (call) or above the strike (put).

series Options sharing identical terms (type of option, underlying stock, strike, and expiration).

settlement date The date when a buyer is required to pay for purchases or when a seller is entitled to payment. Stock settlement is three business days from the transaction. Option settlement is one business day from the transaction.

short hedge Any use of short options to mitigate risk in long stock positions from unfavorable price movement.

short position Status when traders have entered a sale order to open a position in advance of entering a closing buy order. Short positions are closed by entering an offsetting purchase to close order or through expiration of the short option.

short selling A stock strategy when shares of stock are borrowed from a broker and sold to create a short position, hoping value will fall; the short is later closed with a closing purchase transaction.

short straddle The sale of the same number of calls and puts with the same strike and expiration. It becomes profitable when the price of the underlying stock remains within a limited profit zone.

short-term capital gains Profits from investments held for less than 12 months, taxed at ordinary rates.

sideways strategies Any option strategies that become profitable when the underlying stock remains within a narrow trading range.

speculation Capital used to trade short-term profit, including long positions in options, swing trading, or uncovered short selling stock or options.

spread Purchase and sale of options with different strike prices or expiration, or with both.

straddle The purchase and sale of options with the same strike and expiration.

strike The price per share to be paid for 100 shares of stock upon exercise of an option, no matter what the current price per share of the underlying.

support   The lowest trading price within the stock's current trading range.

synthetic position   A strategy when combined positions mimic the price movement of other positions (for example, using options to mirror the price movement of long or short stock).

tax put   The sale of stock at a tax loss with the sale of a put at the same time. The put premium offsets the stock loss; if the put is exercised, the stock is purchased at the striking price.

terms   The standardized terms of option: strike, expiration, type of option (call or put), and the underlying stock.

time value   An option's current premium attributed strictly to the amount of time remaining until expiration, and excluding intrinsic and extrinsic value.

total return   The return from selling a call, capital gain from profit on selling the stock, and dividends earned and received. For short puts, this consists of the capital gain from selling stock, plus the put option received.

trading range   The price range of stock between support and resistance.

uncovered option   The sale of a call not protected by the ownership of 100 shares of the underlying stock, or of a put when the trader is not short 100 shares.

underlying stock   The stock specified in every option contract.

variable hedge   A hedge with both long and short positions, when one side has more options than the other.

vertical spread   A spread with different strikes and identical expiration.

volatility   The degree of change in a stock's market value (historical volatility) or the estimated change in an option's market value to occur in the future (implied volatility).

wash sale rule   A tax rule banning the deduction of a loss if the position is reopened within 30 days from the date of the sale.

wasting asset   An asset that declines in value. An option, for example, has a limited life and experiences time decay and, upon expiration, becomes worthless.

writer   The trader who sells an option.

Index

U

U.S. Steel, 84-85
uncovered puts, 187-191
underlying security, 8
Union Pacific, 125-127, 163-165
United Parcel Service, 90-93
uptrend, 65

V

volatility
    market, 173-174
    option 168-172
    trading, 170-172
    trends, 186

W

Wal-Mart, 5, 180-181, 191-192

Y

Yahoo!, 65, 71-72

FINANCIAL TIMES

In an increasingly competitive world, it is quality
of thinking that gives an edge—an idea that opens new
doors, a technique that solves a problem, or an insight
that simply helps make sense of it all.

We work with leading authors in the various arenas
of business and finance to bring cutting-edge thinking
and best-learning practices to a global market.

It is our goal to create world-class print publications
and electronic products that give readers
knowledge and understanding that can then be
applied, whether studying or at work.

To find out more about our business
products, you can visit us at www.ftpress.com.